Therapy for Thought
A Visual Journey into the Mandelbrot Set

Vinayaki's Valley

Alex Hanley

Designed by Alex Hanley

A Platinum Pirate Production

ISBN-10: 0615801390
ISBN-13: 978-0615801391

www.therapy4thought.com

Disclaimer

These series of books do not map the entire Mandelbrot Set; it is just some key points for further exploration. This book reflects the author's views and opinions related to his understanding of his own universe and should not be taken literally. The author does not claim to be credited in mathematics nor philosophy, and is not responsible for your loss of sanity when your mind opens up to infinite thought from staring at the images too long.

Enjoy☺

The Mandelbrot Set was named after Benoit Mandelbrot in 1980.
"The M-Set" was coined by Arthur C. Clarke in the book: "The Colours of Infinity-*The Beauty and Power of Fractals*"

From the author

All images in this book are originated within one sector of the Mandelbrot Set, and have not been manipulated in any way. These images were found simply by magnifying in on specific quadrants hidden inside Vinayaki's Valley.

Vinayaki – Elephant headed Hindu goddess

Coordinates for these images will not be offered in this book because they look like this:
-0.281,188,194,519,886,733,063,607,959,194,724,330,205,137,19…
+0.009,334,248,932,704,302,241,058,732,984,663,759,687,754,56…

Unfortunately, many images did not make it into this book and I encourage you to explore on your own.

This book should be used as motivation for further exploration of fractals and especially the Mandelbrot Set.

For the graphic presentations of the frame by frame journeys, I specifically planned the journey to end with a self-similar copy of the Mandelbrot Set to show you a point at which we fall into a singularity trap that at its edge will keep growing exponentially. However, we could deep field dive forever, taking an infinite amount of different routes and each self-similar image builds upon the previous images. Within only a few magnifications, you will be at a point in the M-Set that no other human being has ever explored before.

The visual representation of The M-Set was not invented, but discovered, only with the assistance of an IBM computer back in 1980. Their computer's ability to handle the large amount of repetitive calculations could easily be done on any basic computer today. Computers can now handle many more calculations (iterations) at much faster rates, providing us with greater detailed renderings. There are many different fractal programs out on the web today, but most of them are used for artistic purposes and are not capable of magnifying to such great depths.

Although the journeys will seem as if we are "diving" into a third dimensional space; when in fact we are only magnifying in on the outlining detail of the M-Set. All images in this book actually lie somewhere in between dimensions. It may seem to occupy an entire two dimensional plane, say points on an (X,Y) graph, but it has no depth. For example, if we are only magnifying in on the fractions of coordinates on a two dimensional graph, and the plotted coordinates just get infinitely closer and closer toward each other, with the numbers getting smaller and smaller. We get an over flow of the two dimensional space, but it will not spill over into the third dimensional space since we are only magnifying in on the infinitely detailed, space-filling curve of the M-Set.

Could the M-Set be a map or code from another dimension that we cannot decipher within our three dimensional existence?

What is a fraction of a whole dimension?

Part I

A frame by frame journey

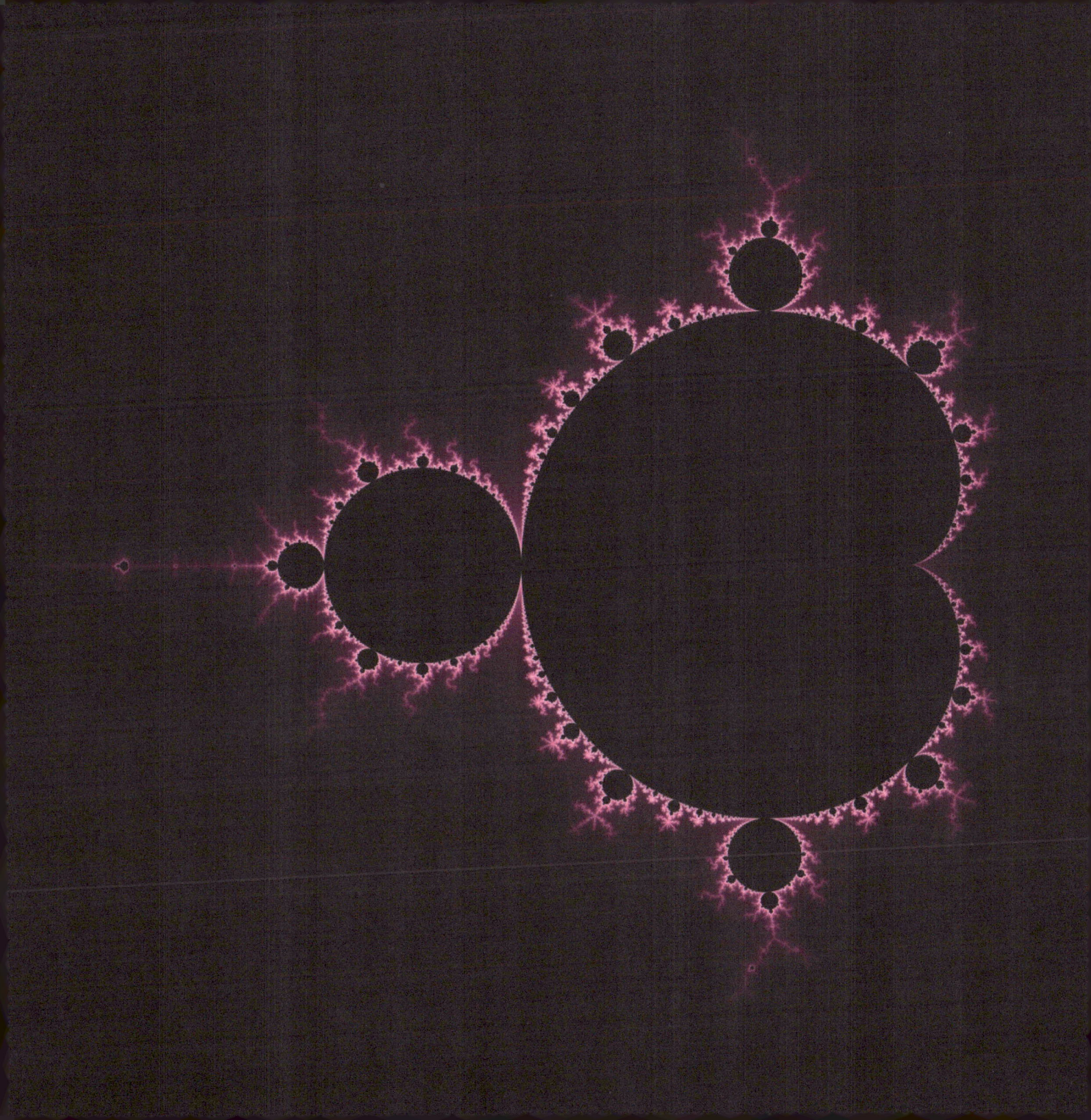

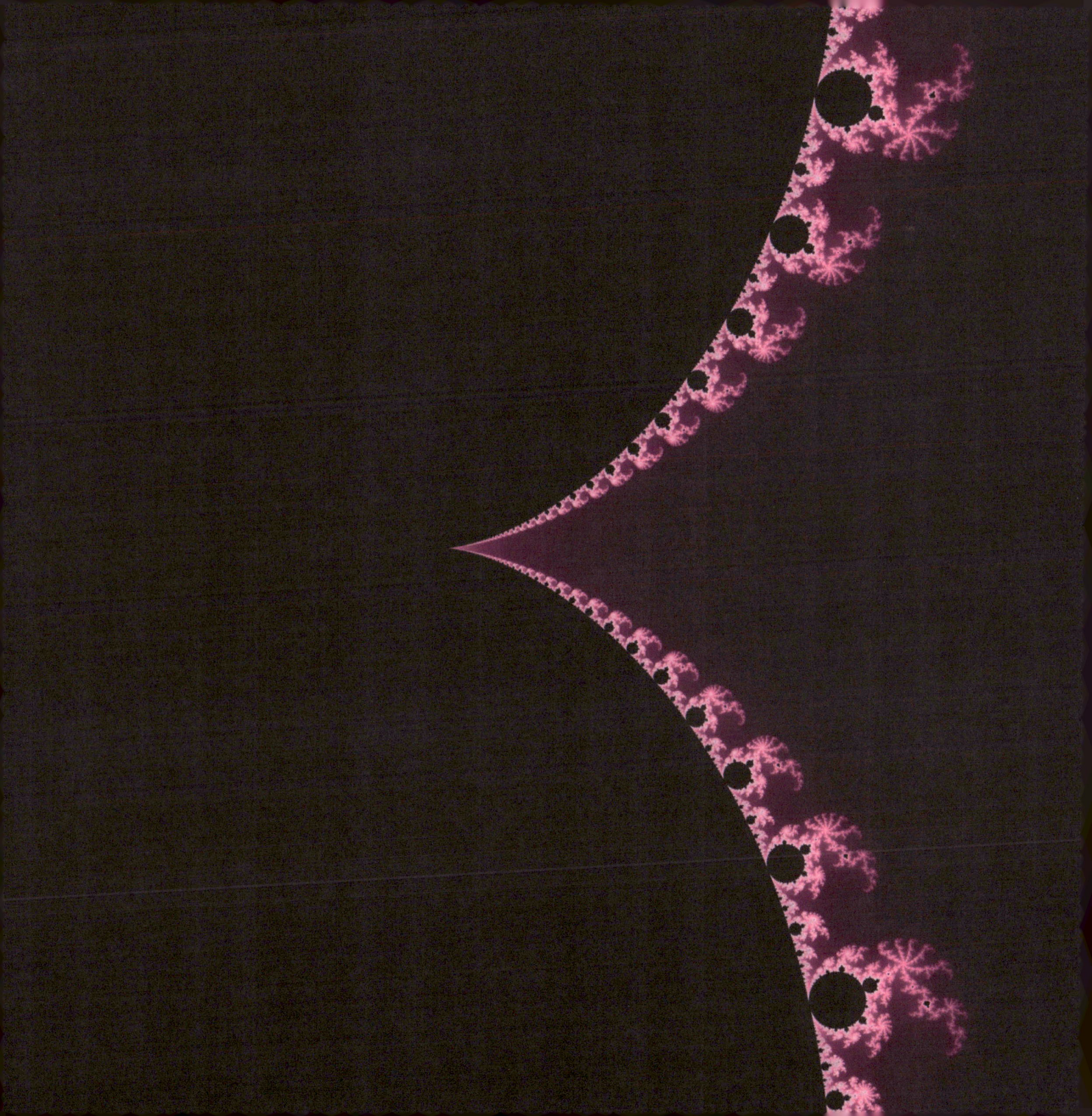

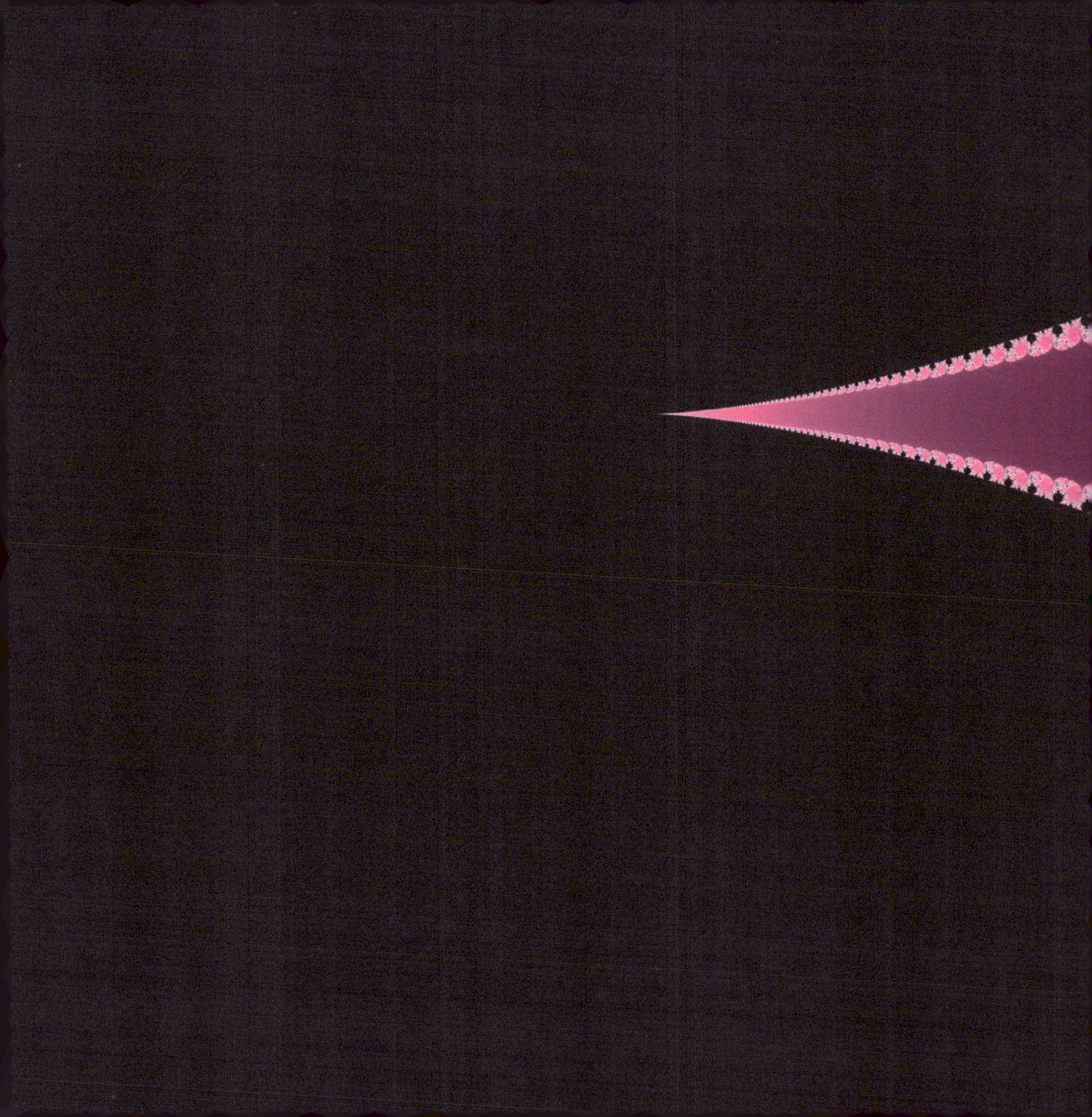

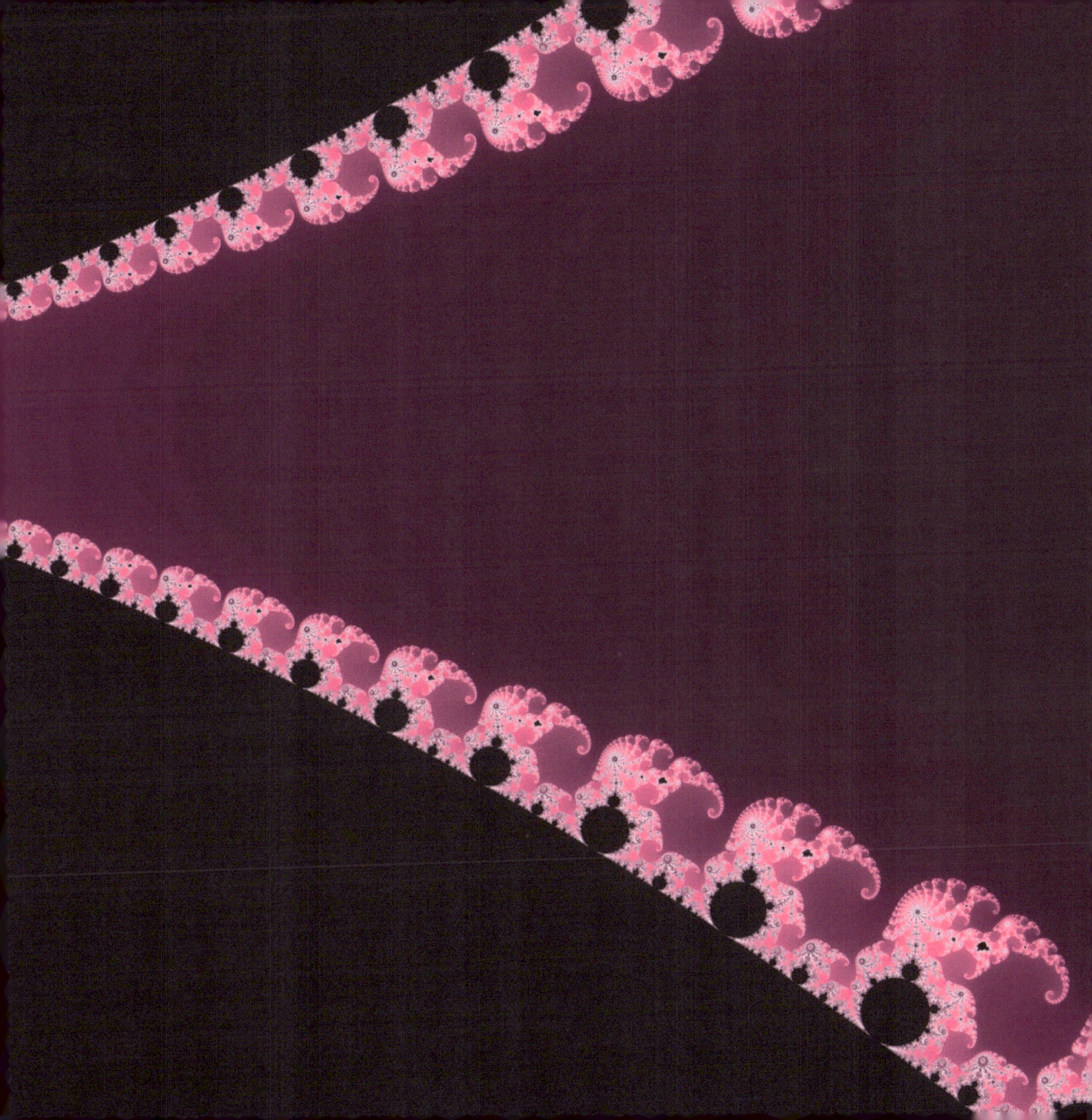

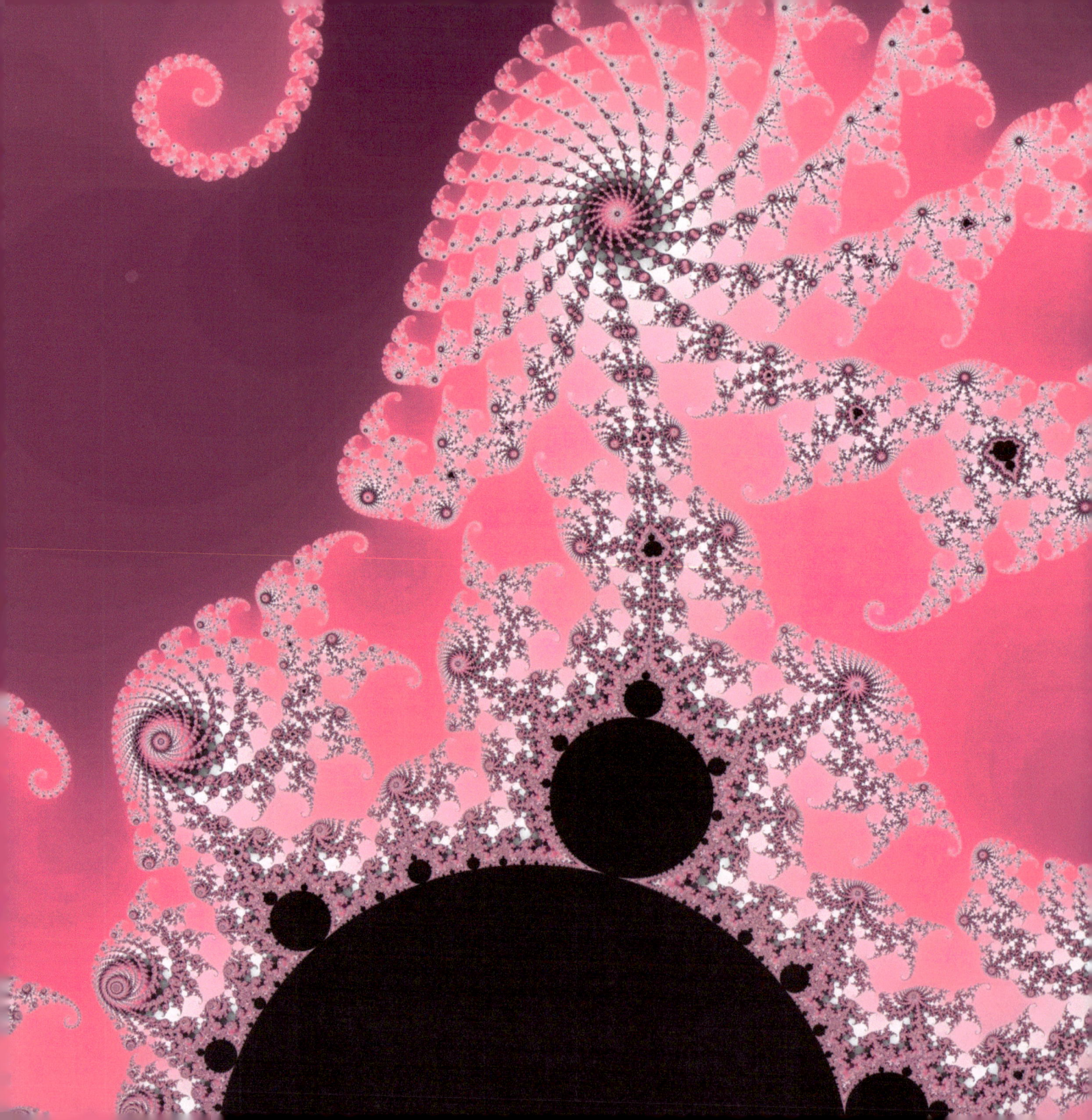

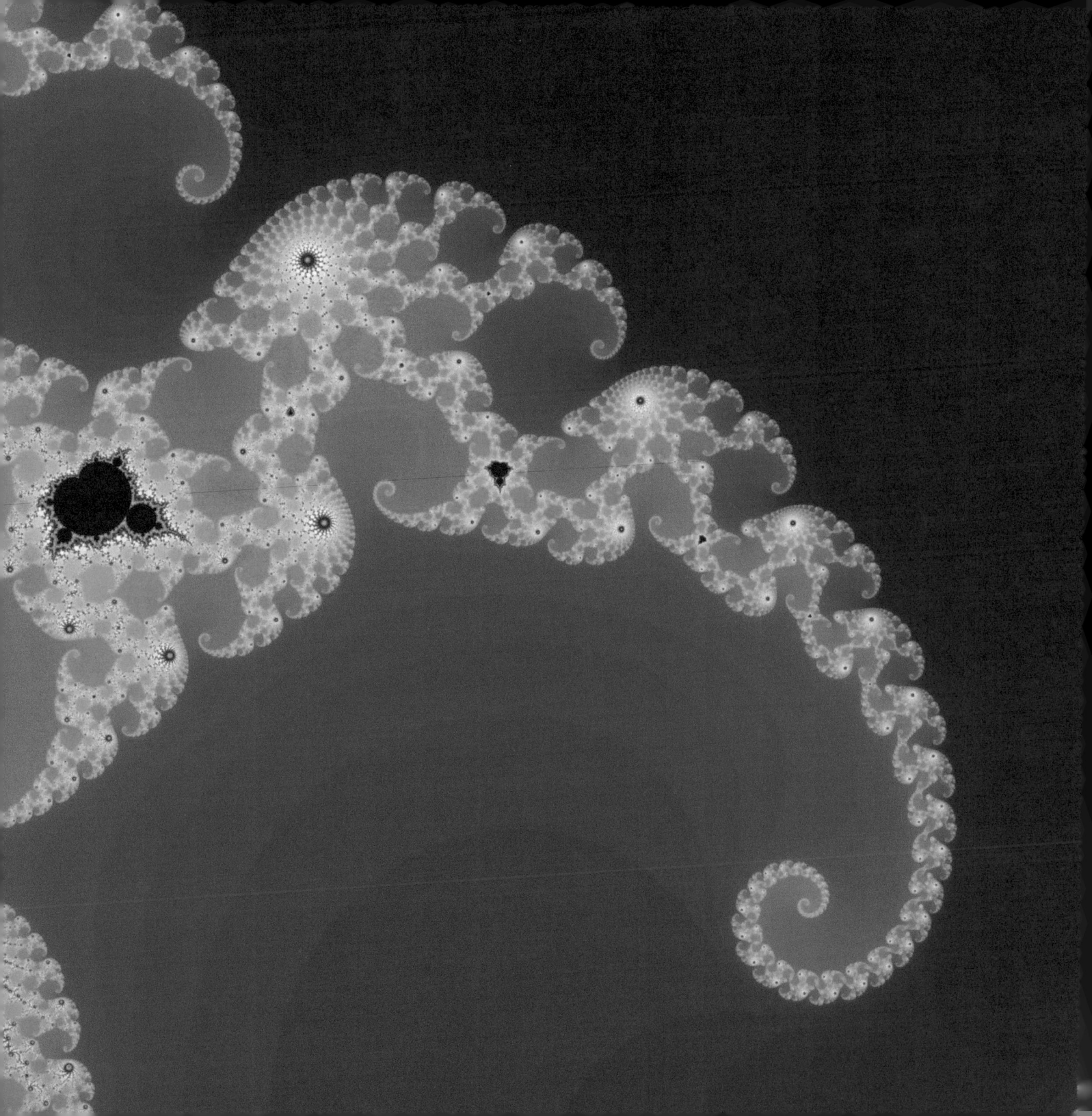

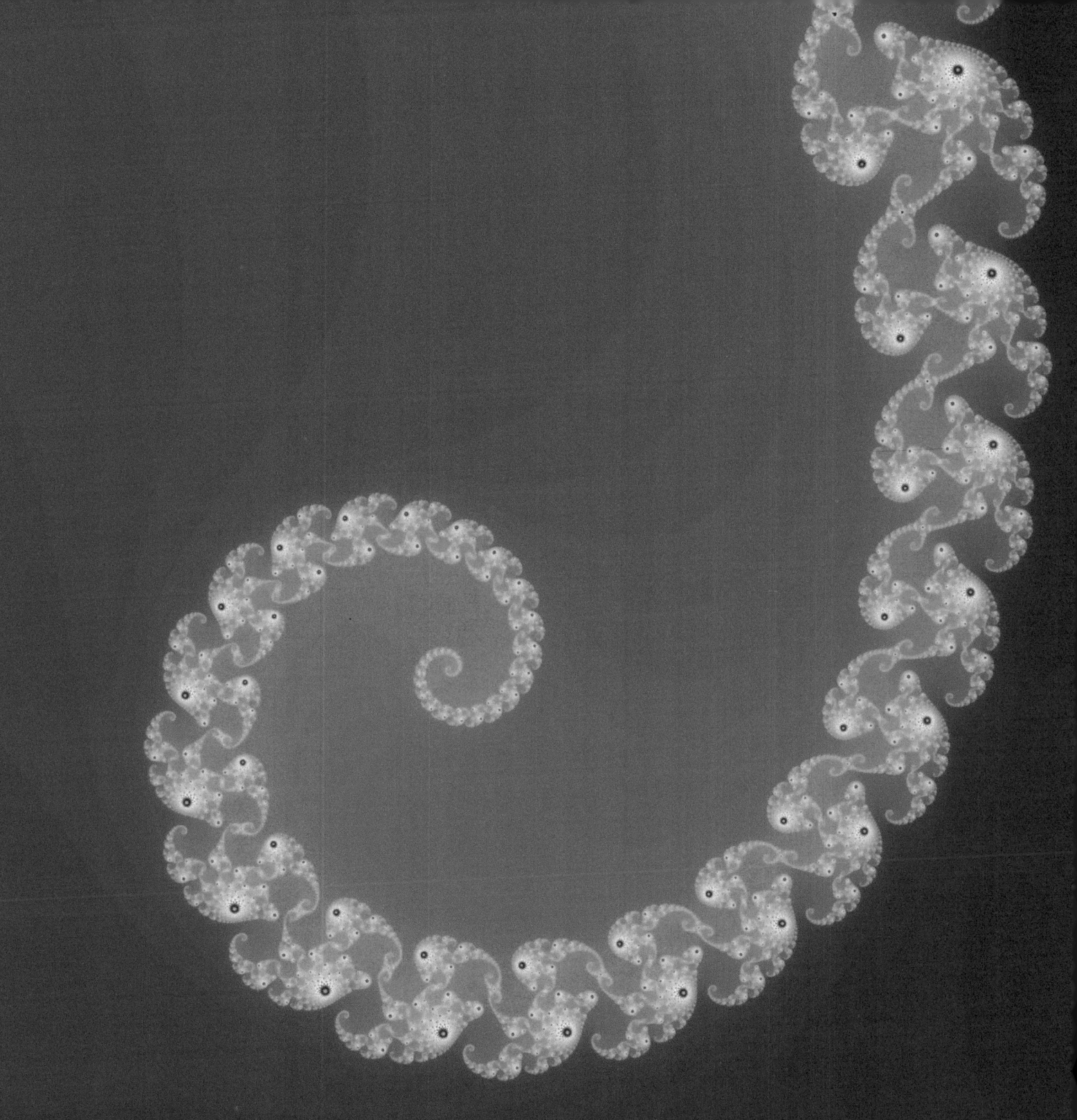

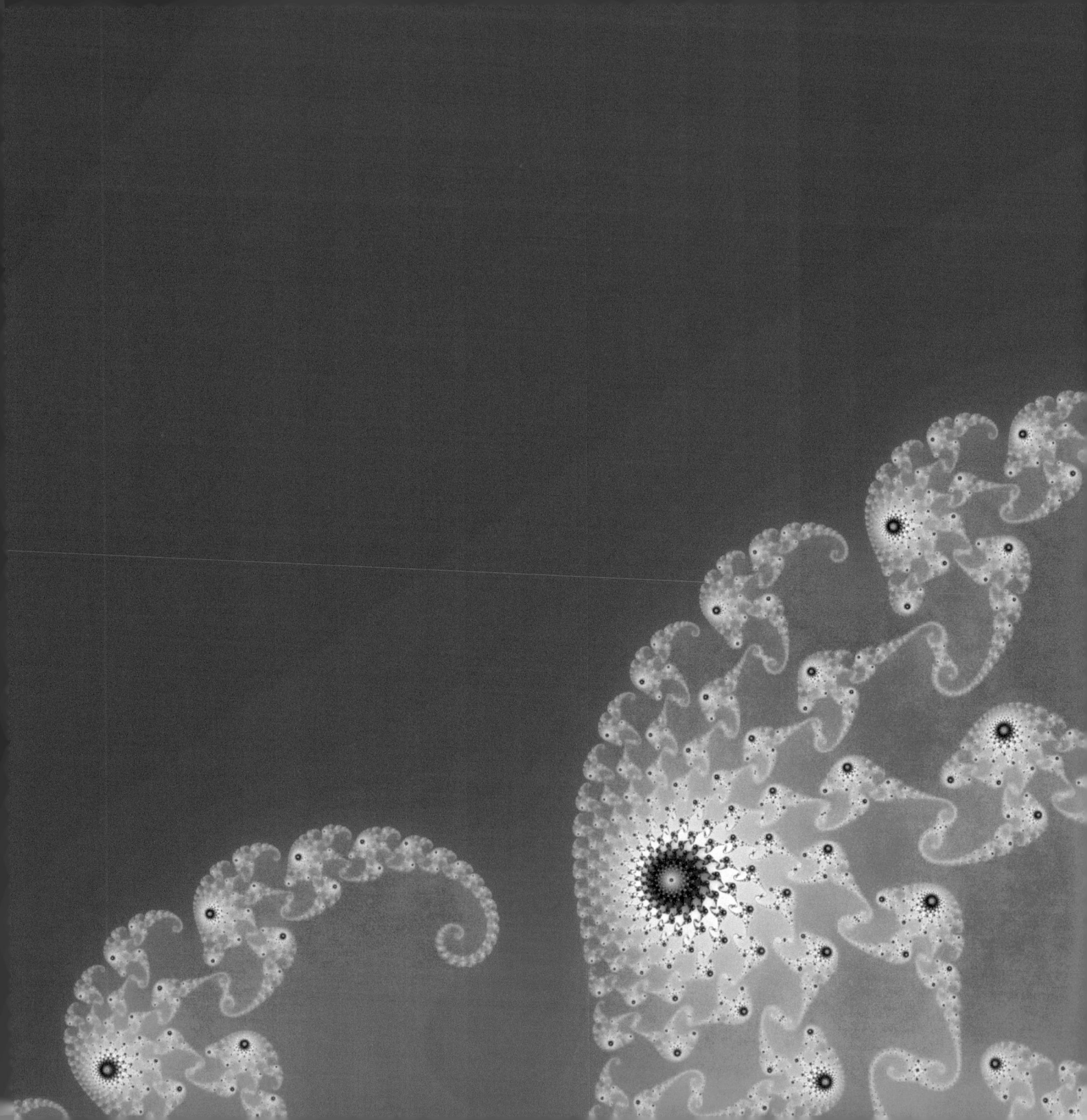

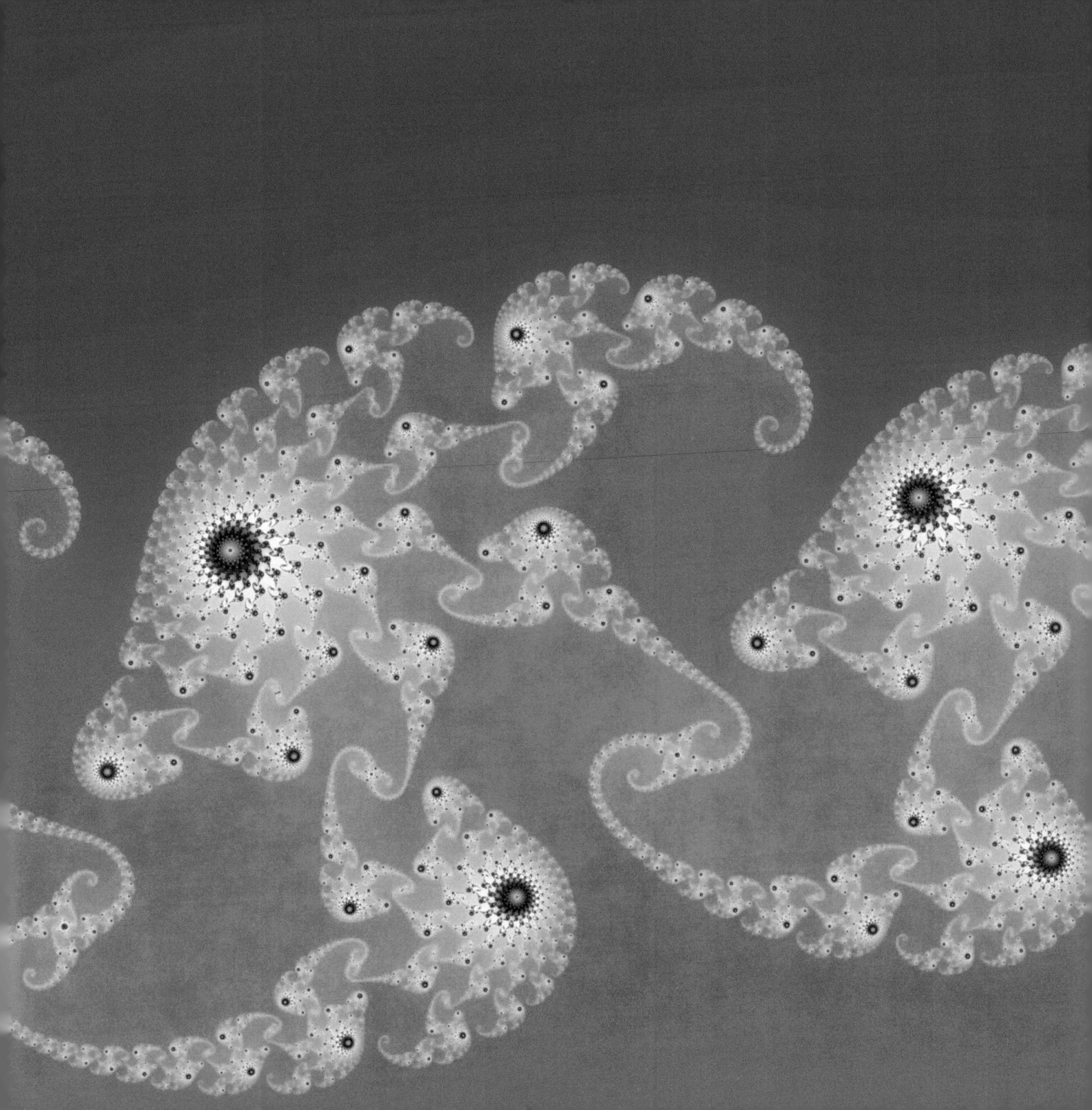

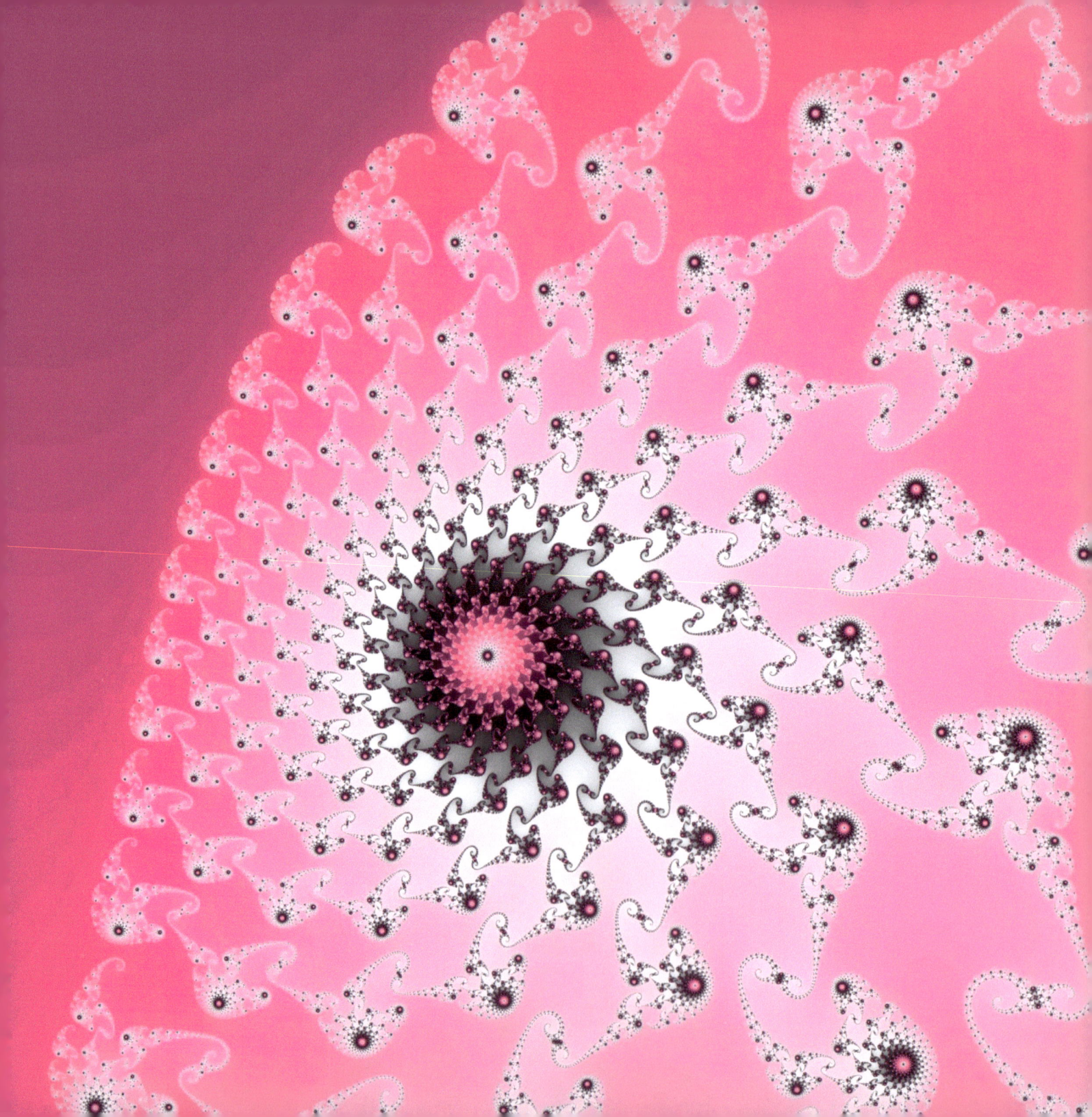

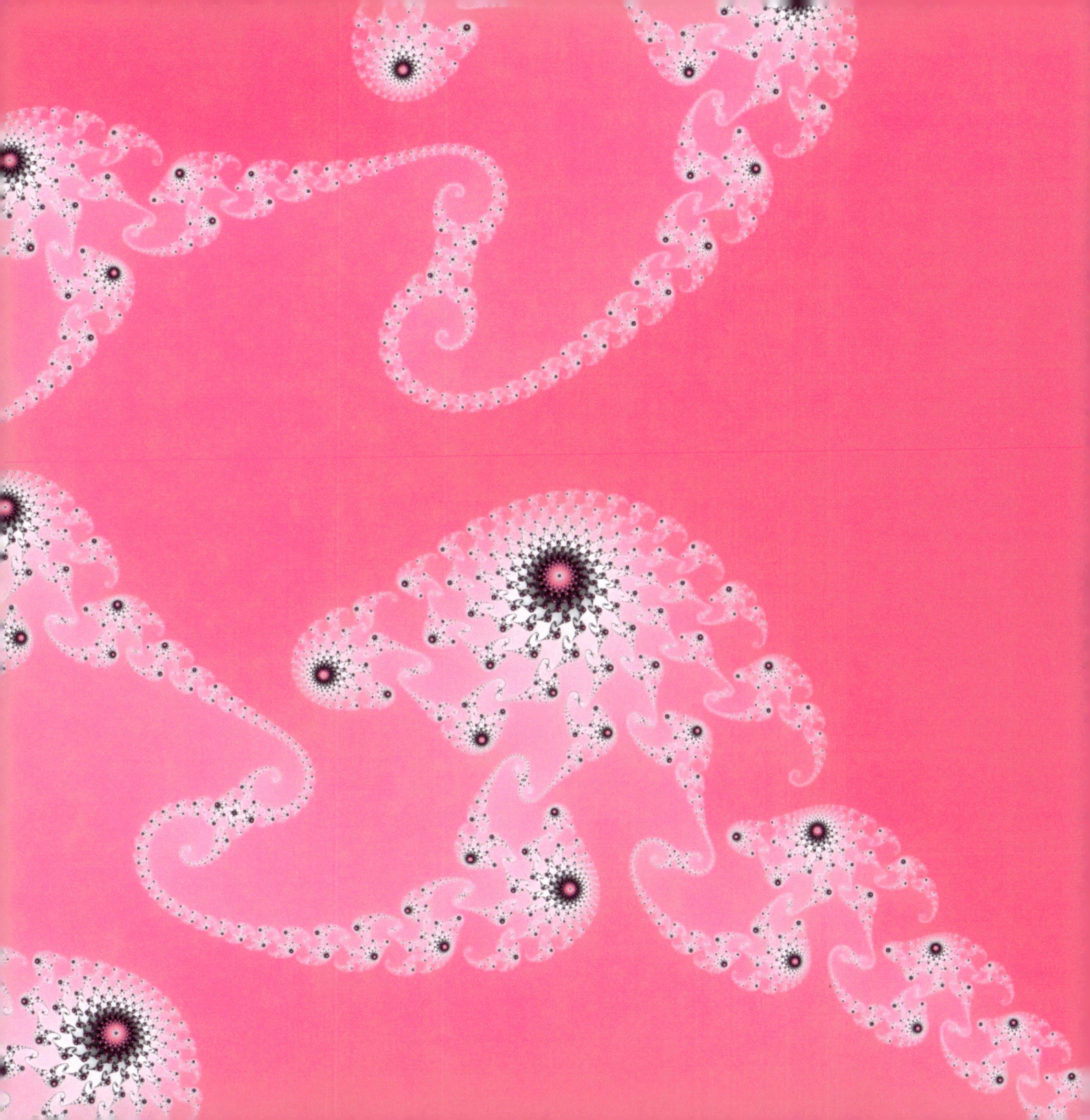

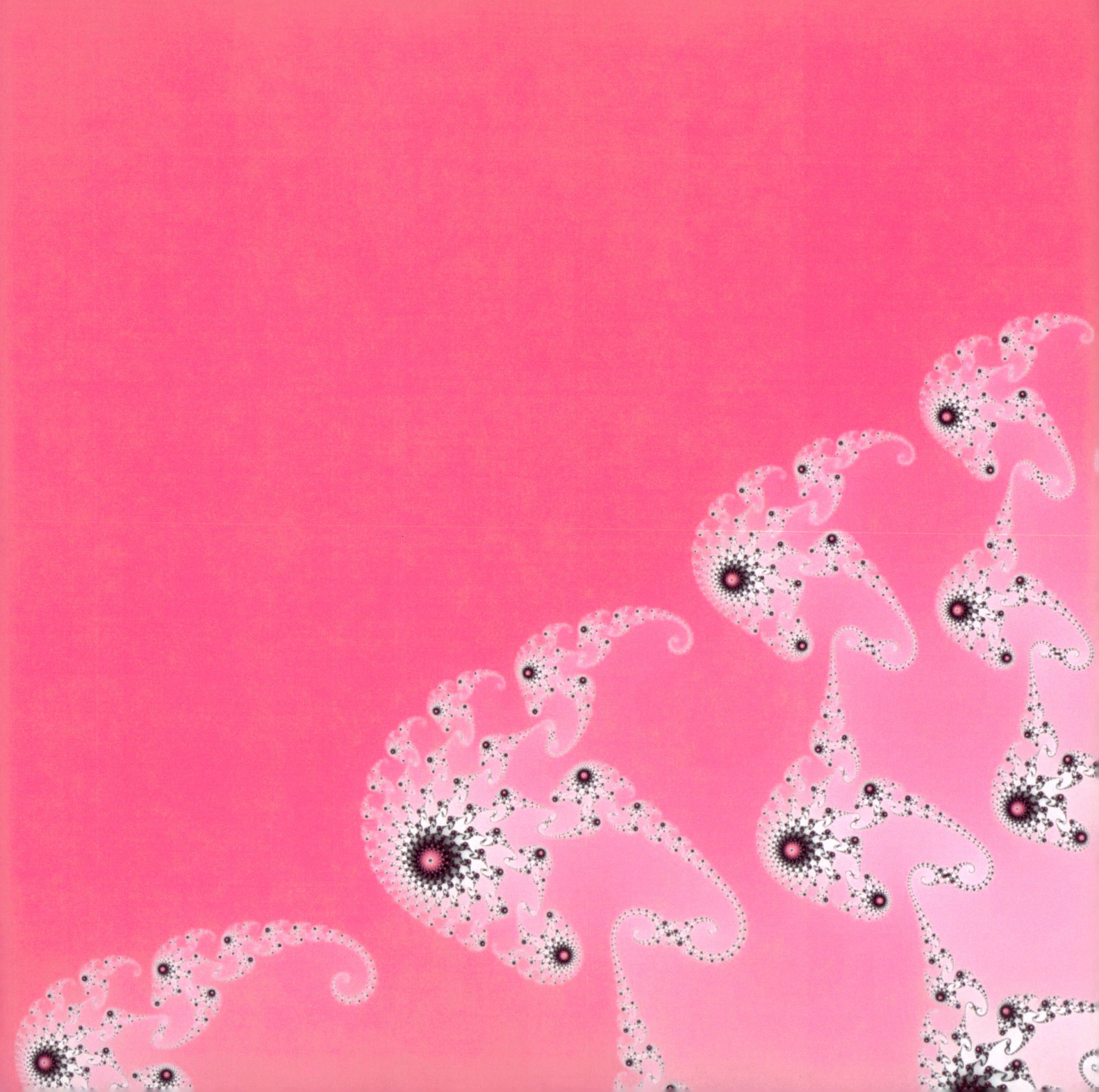

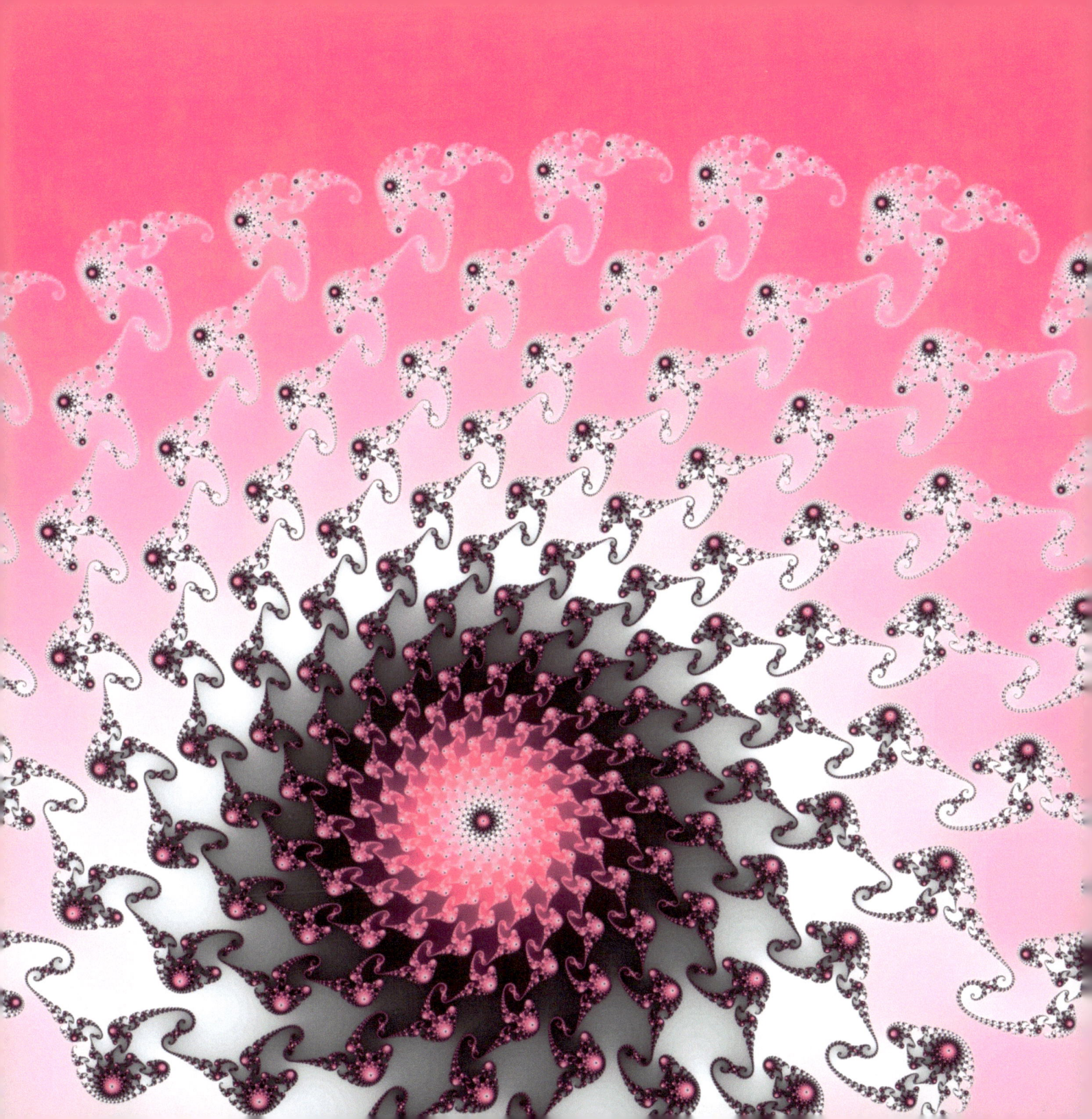

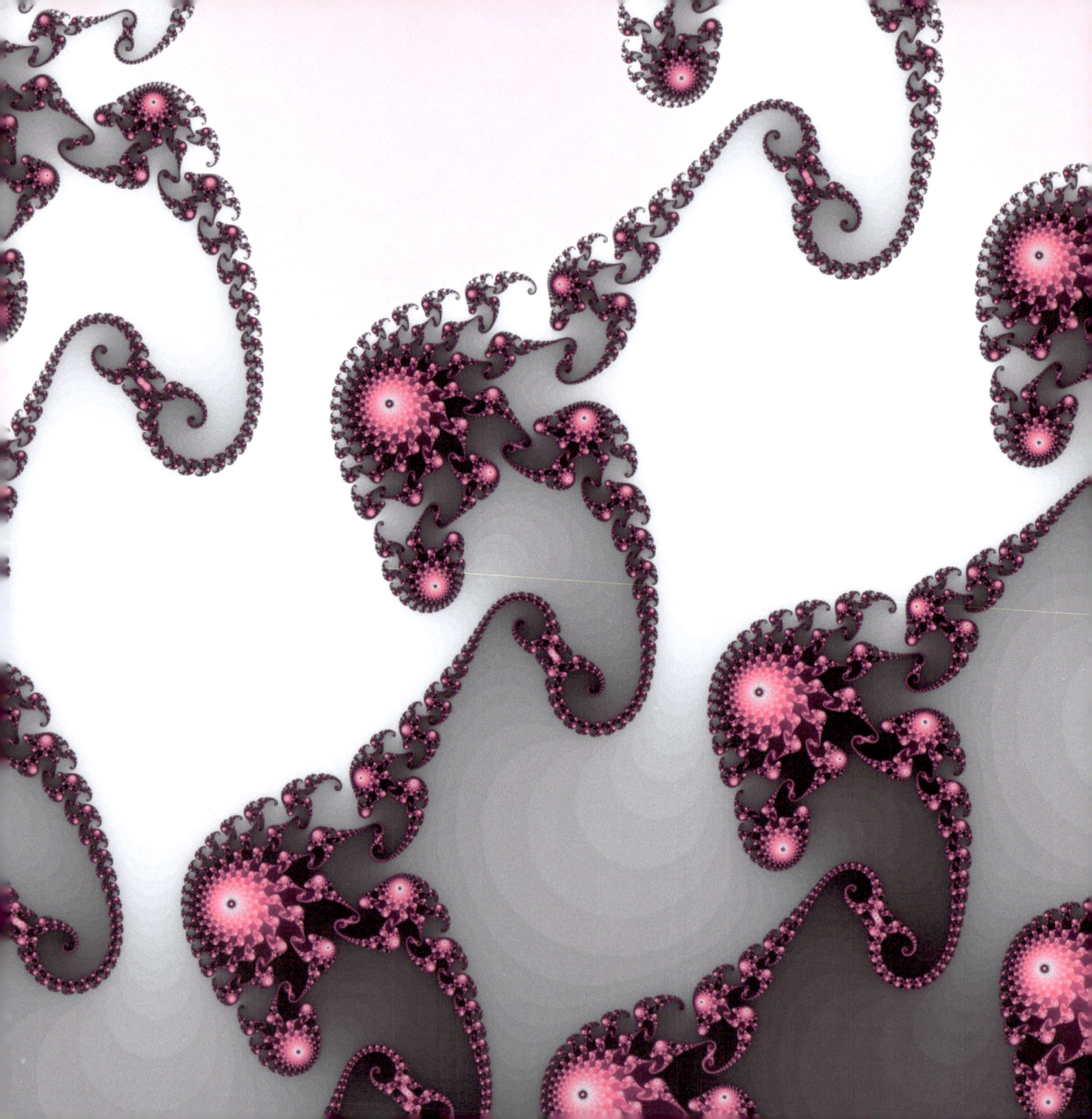

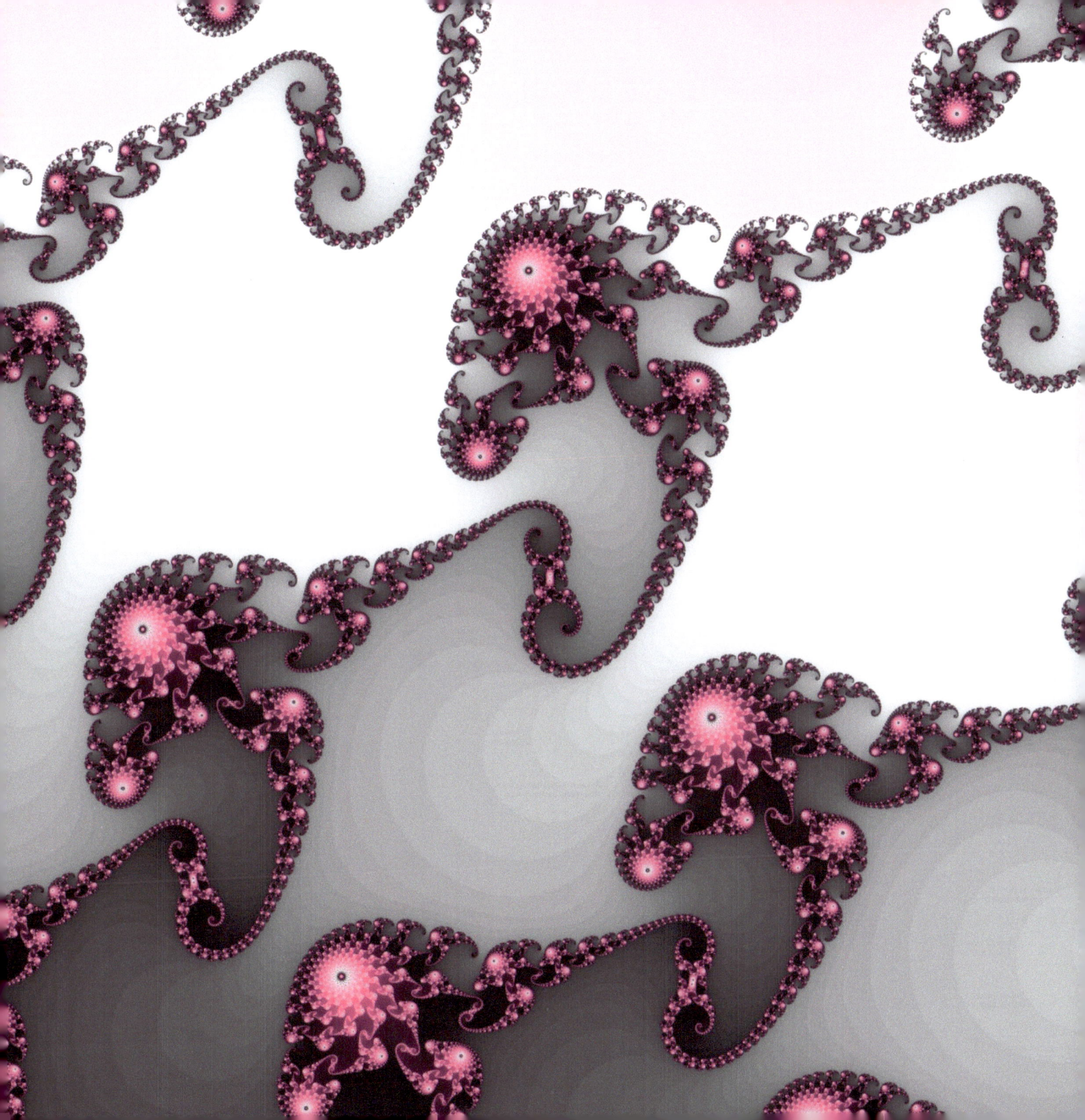

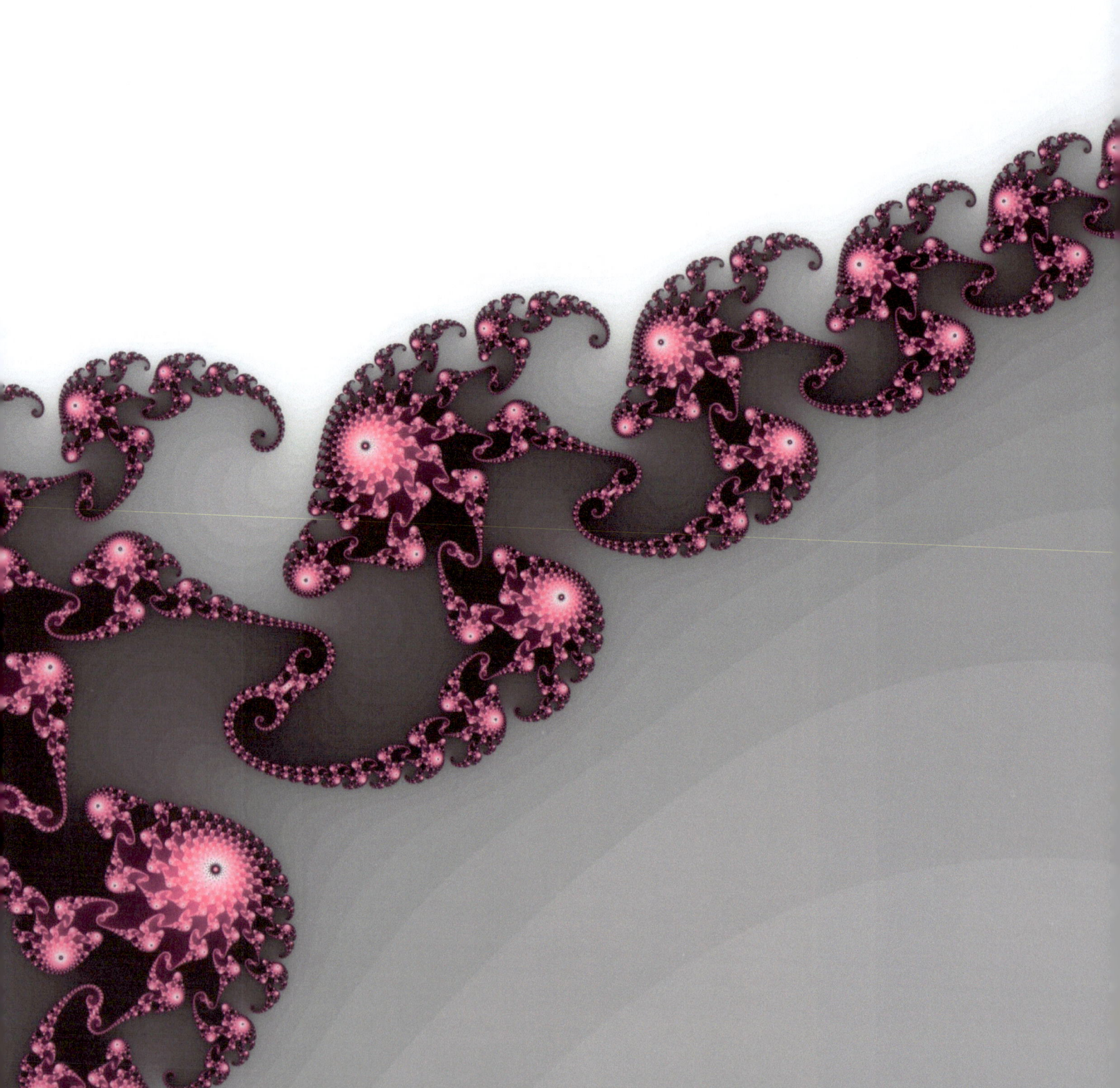

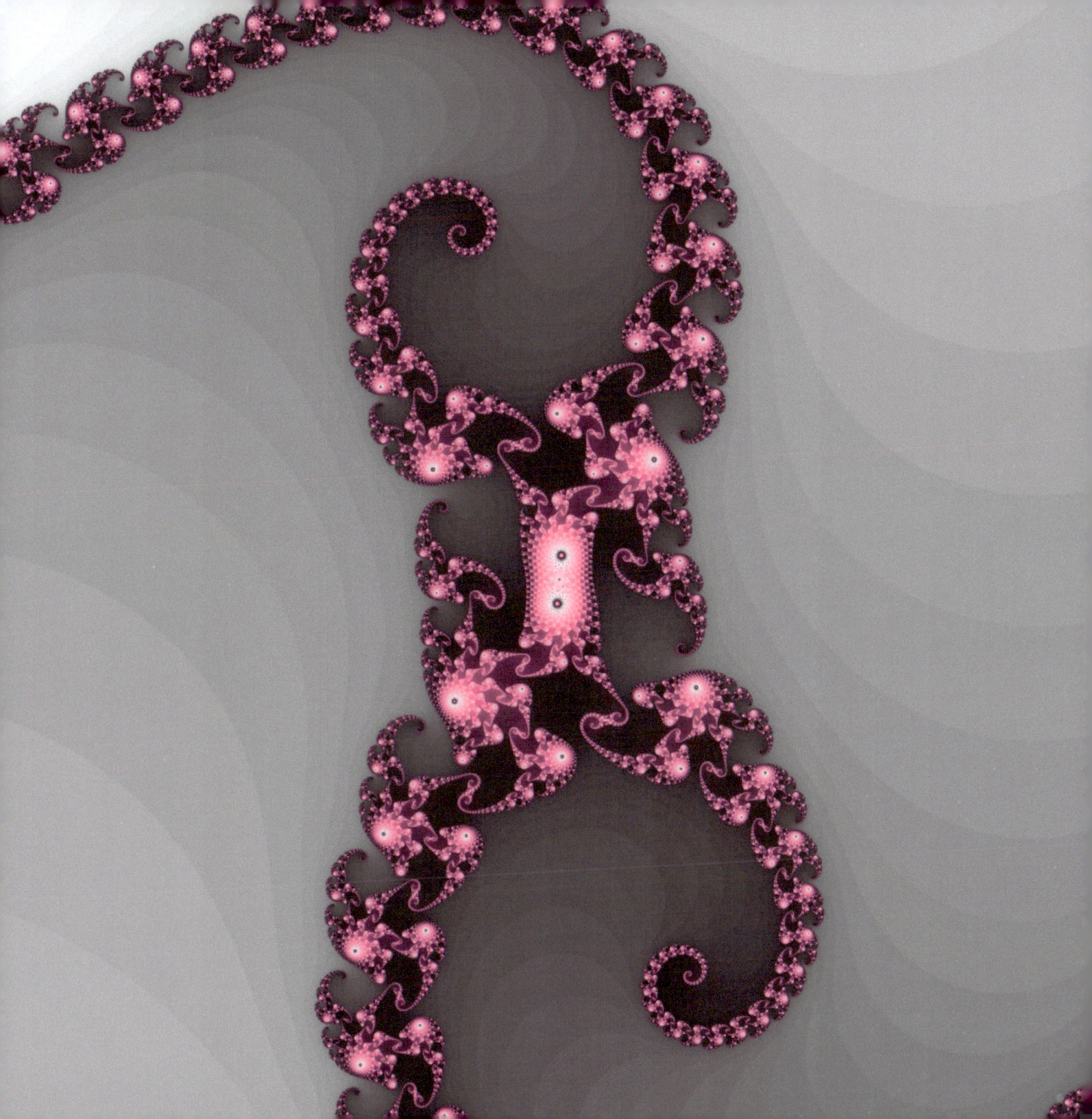

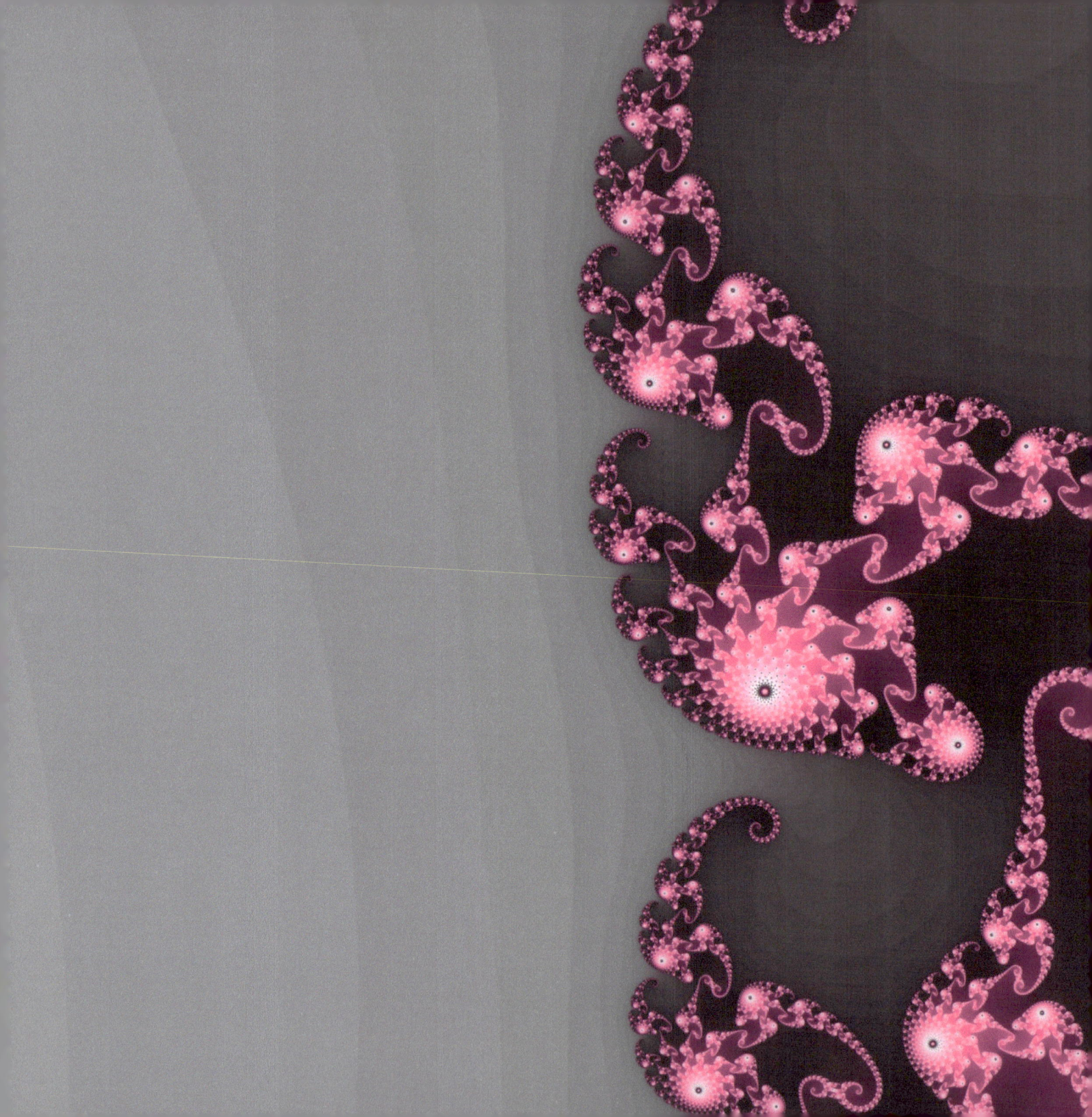

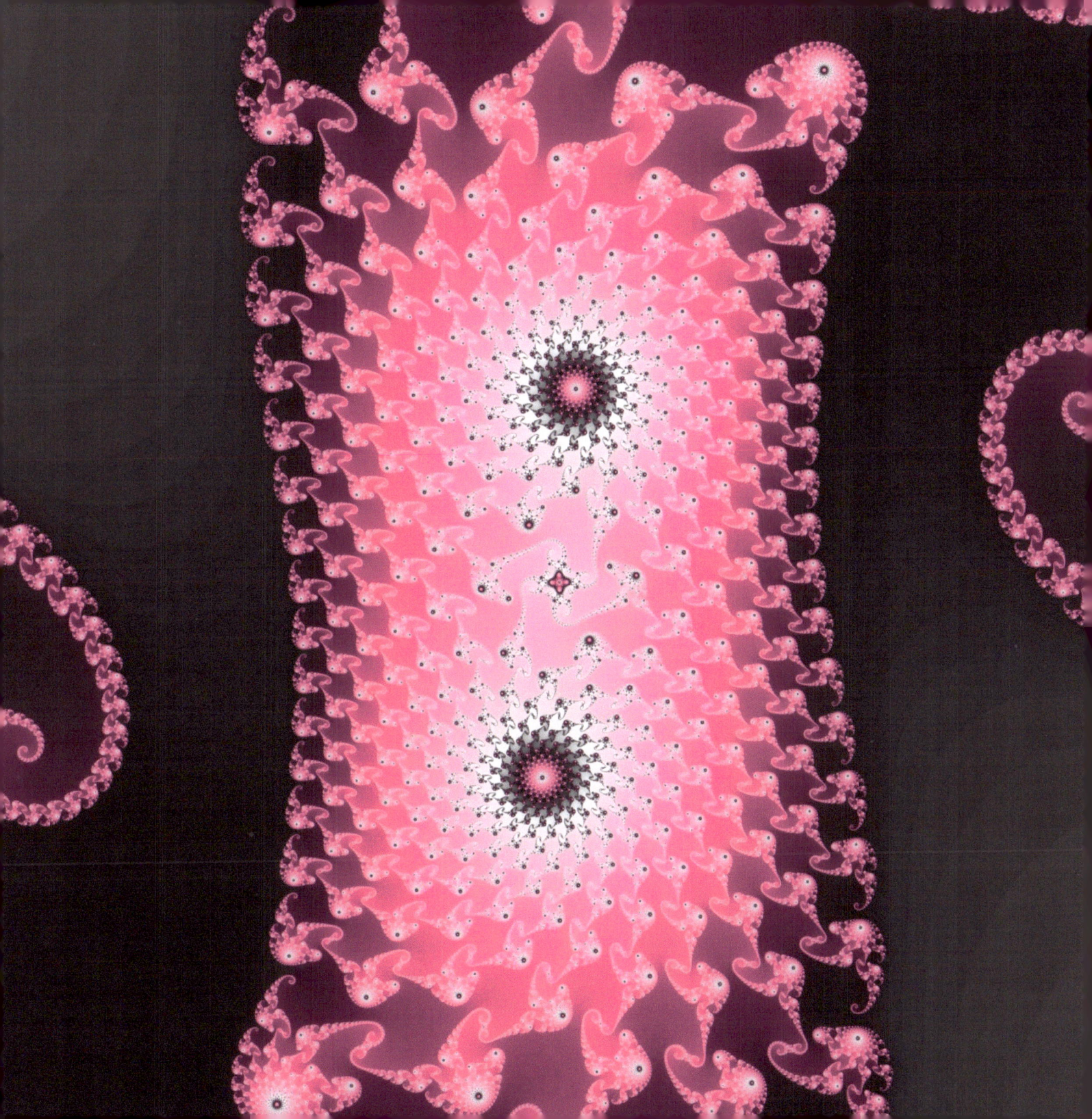

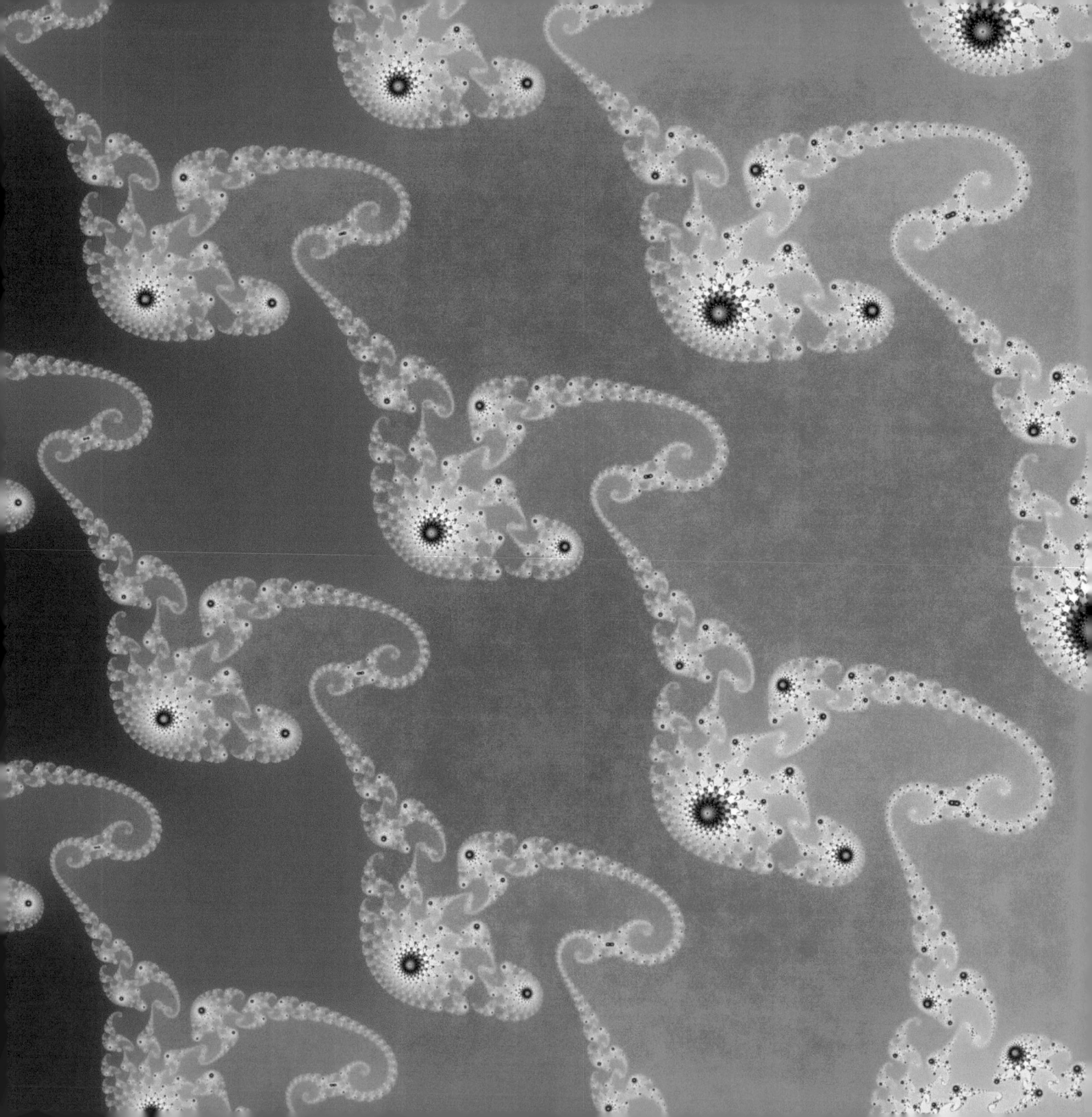

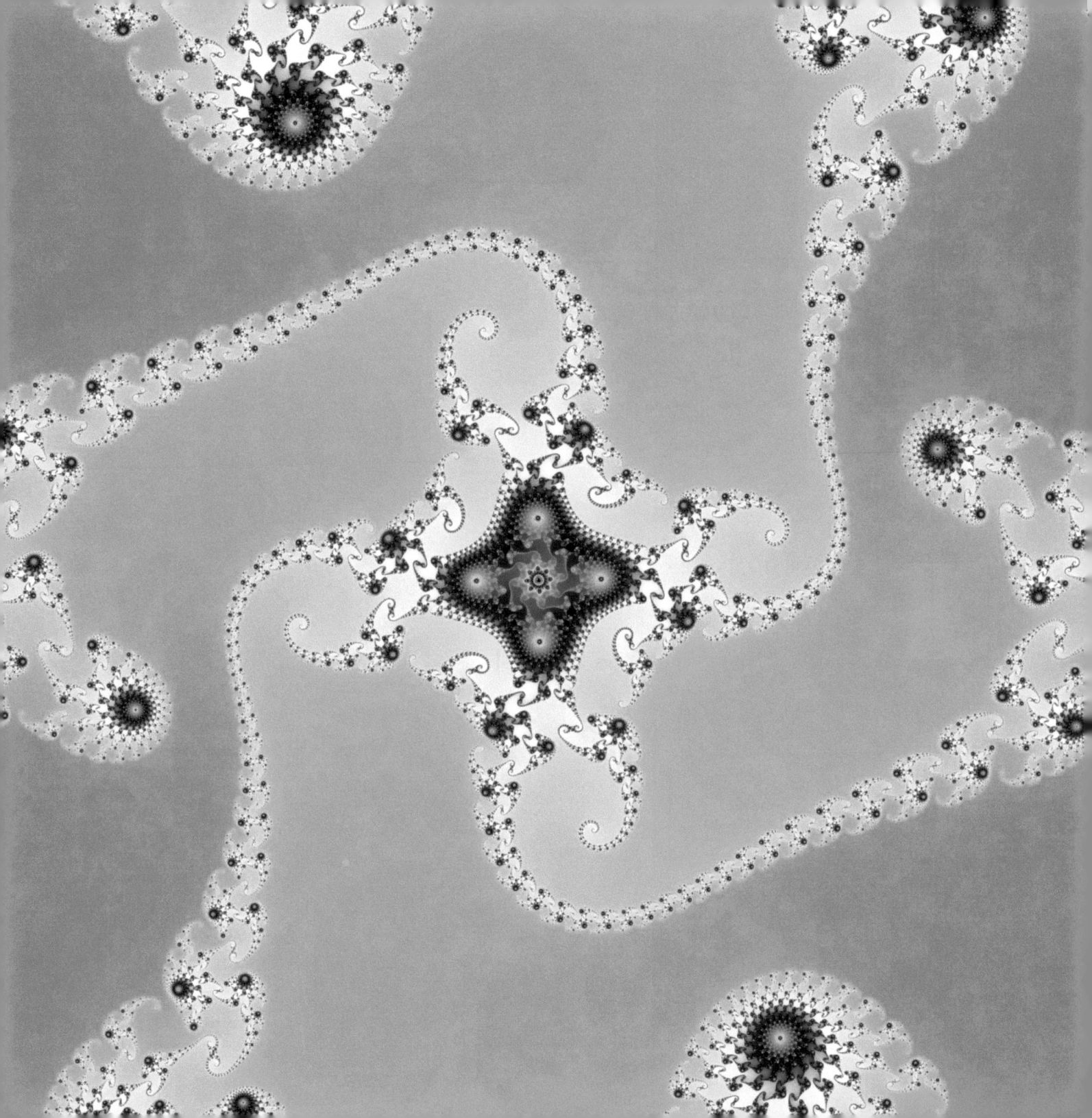

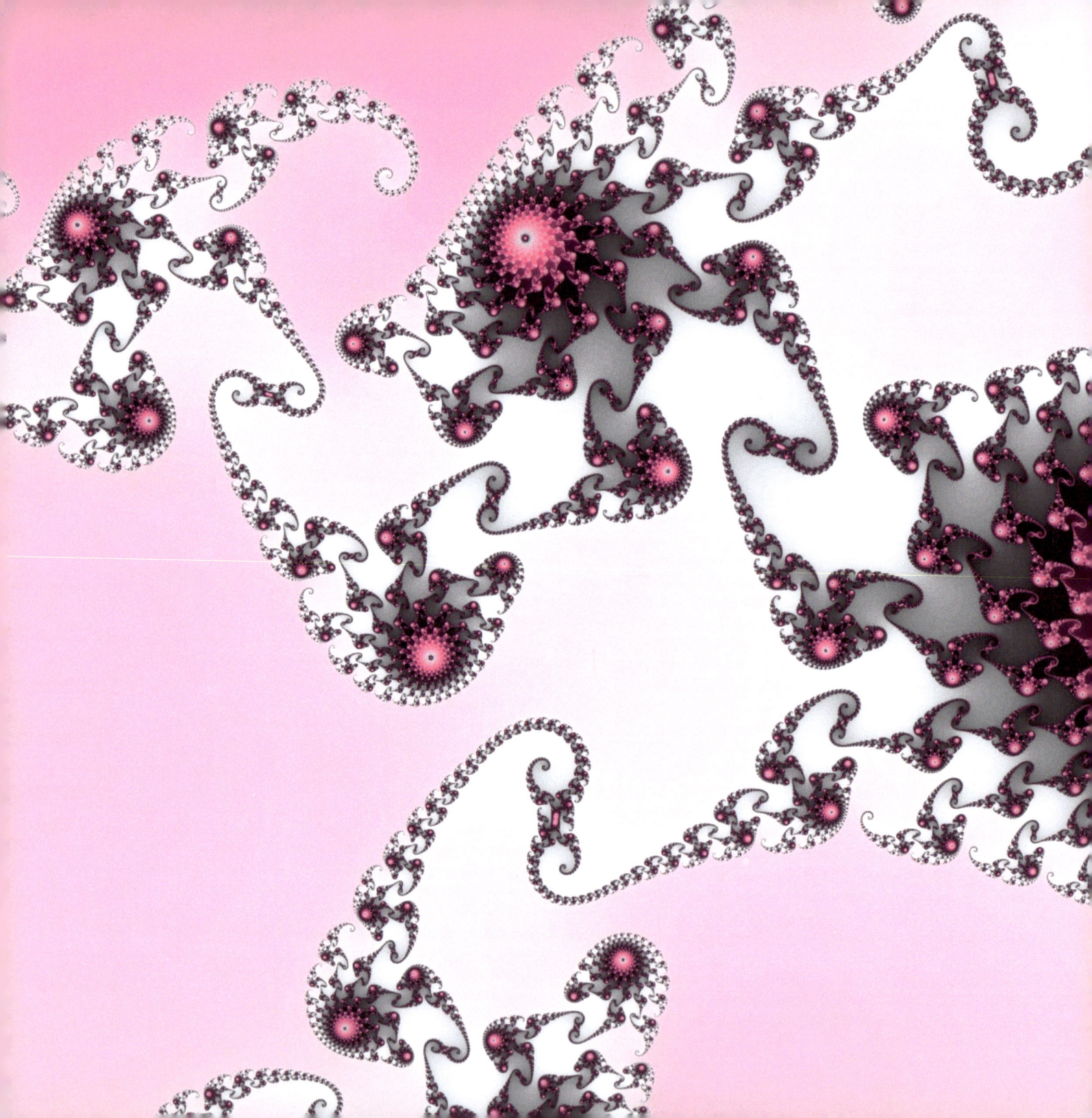

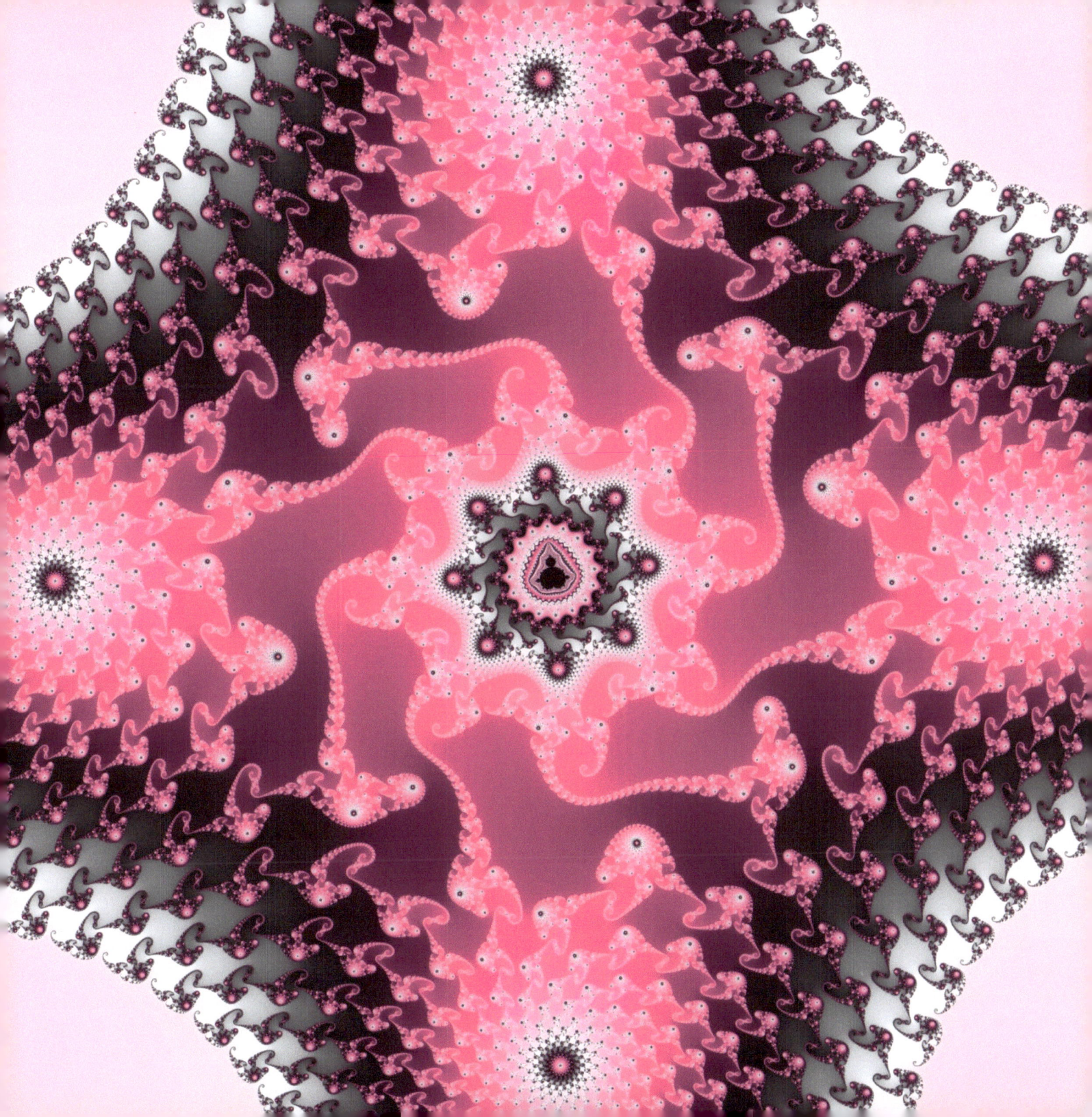

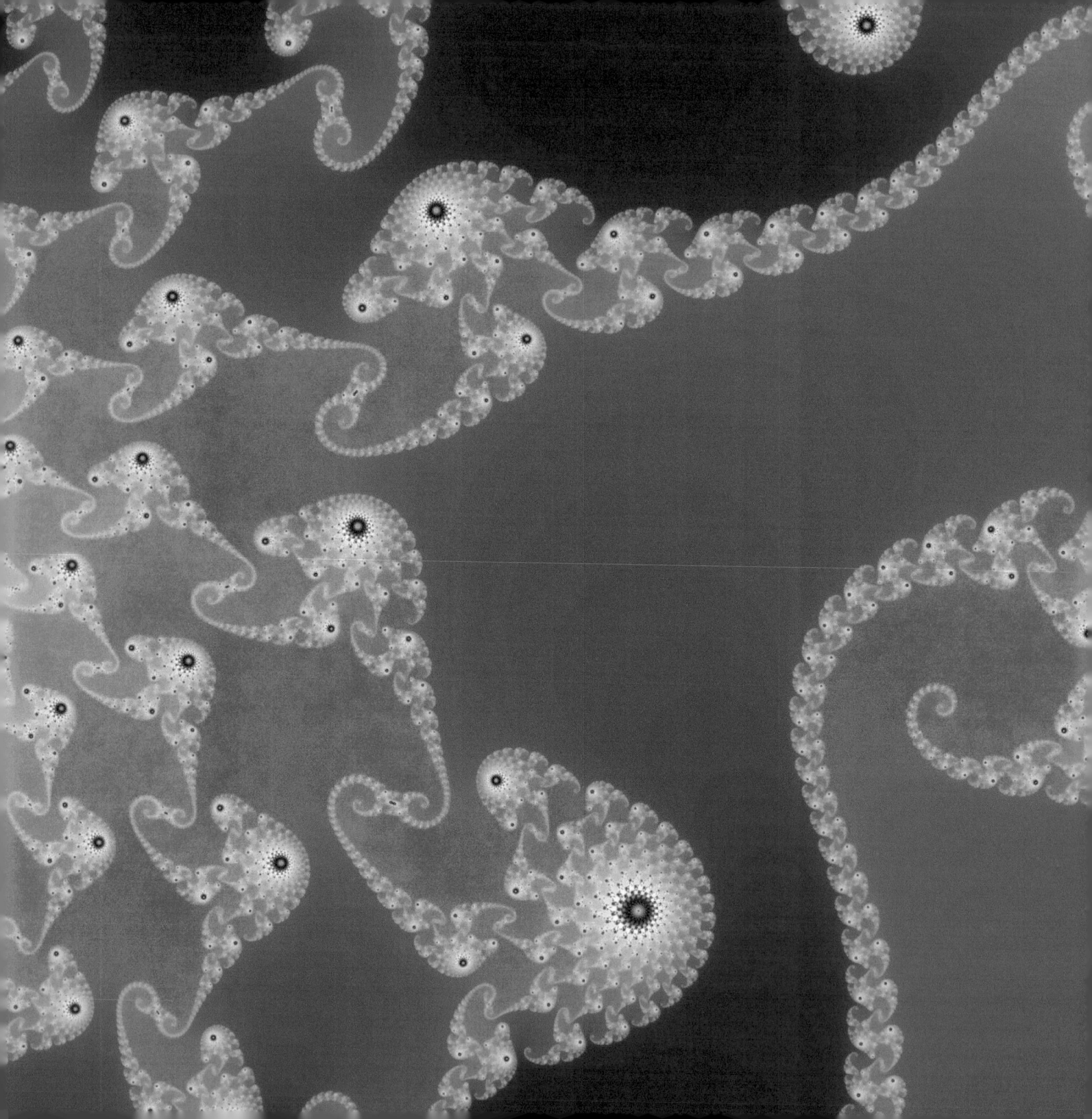

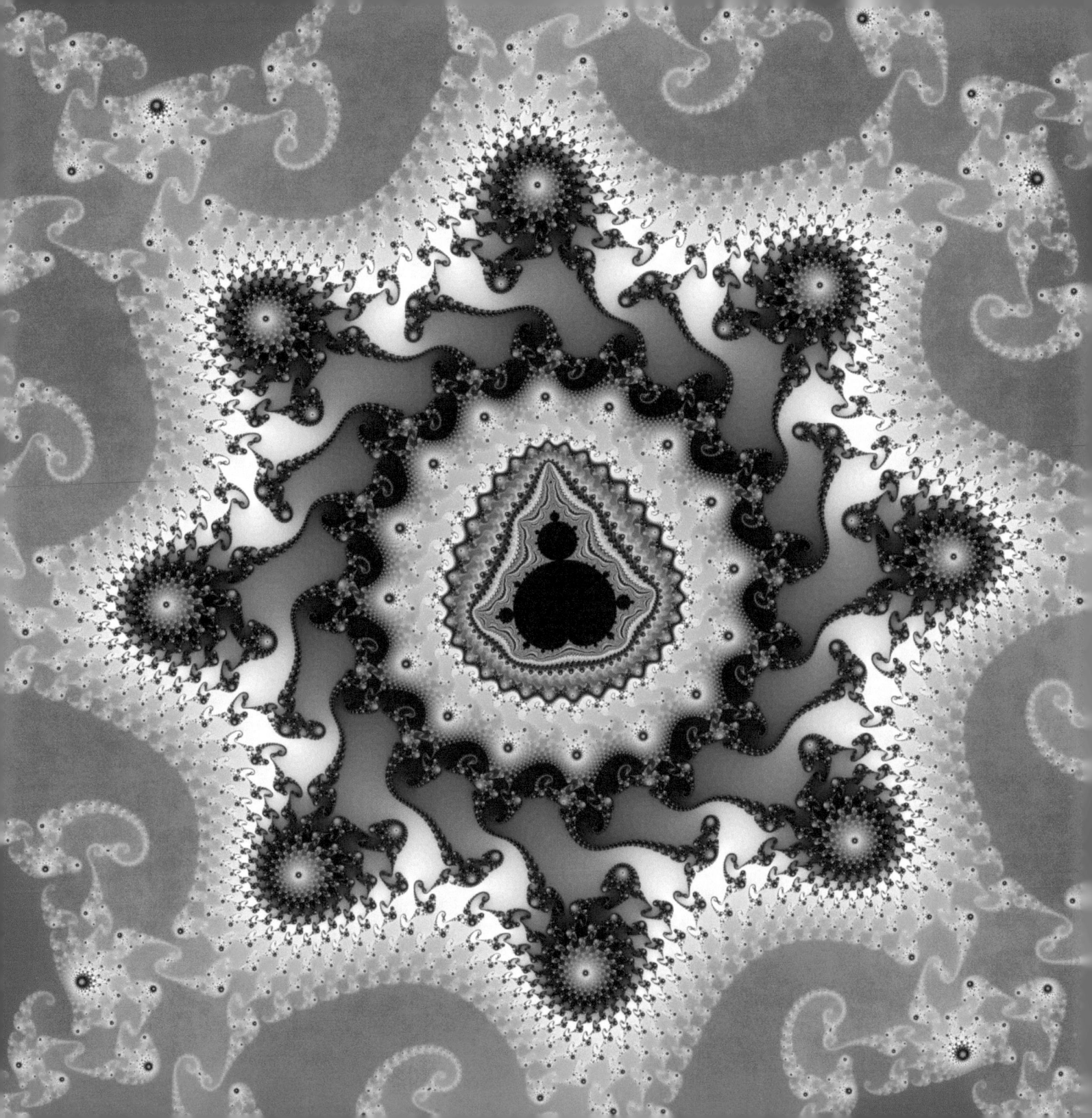

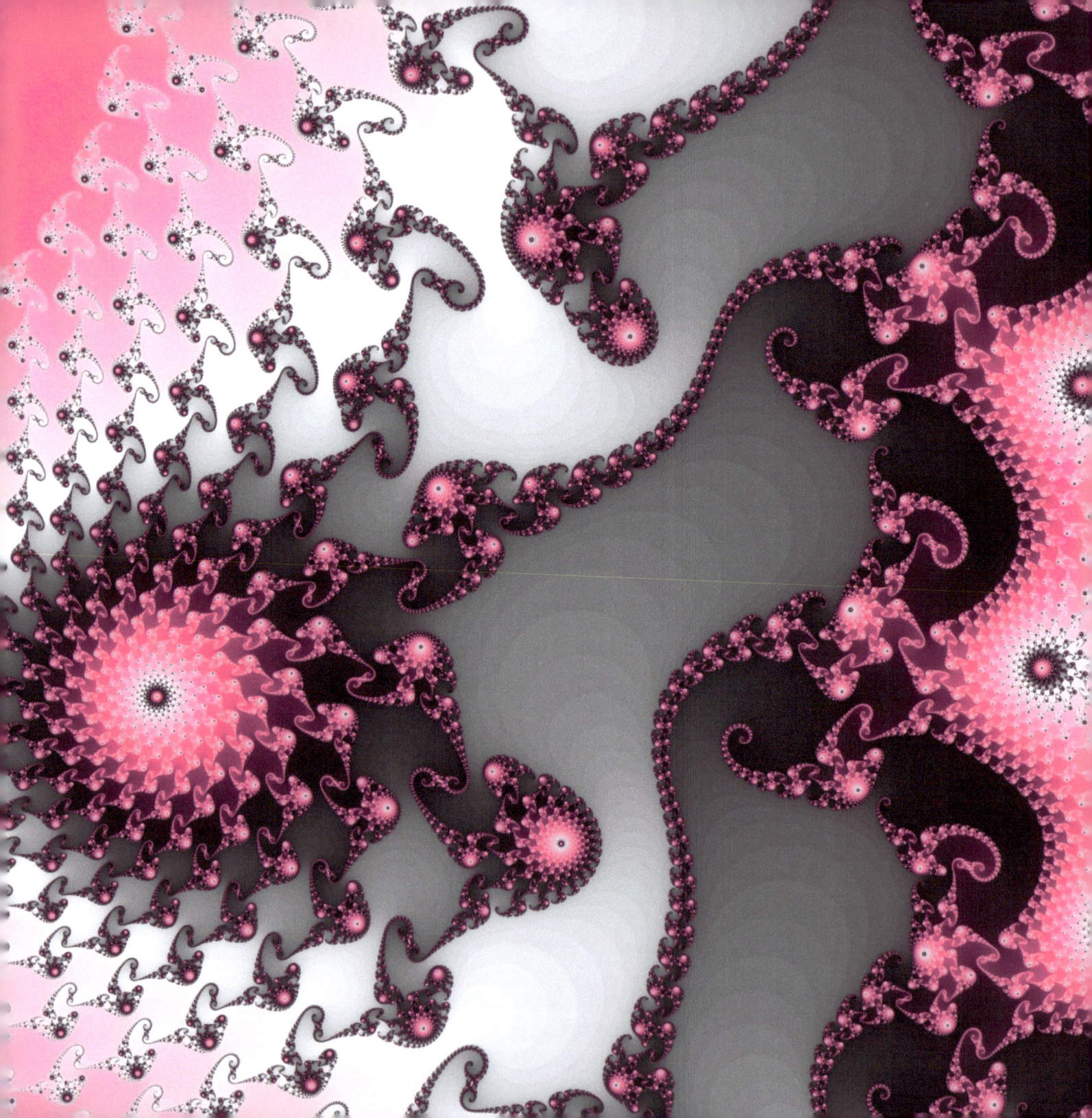

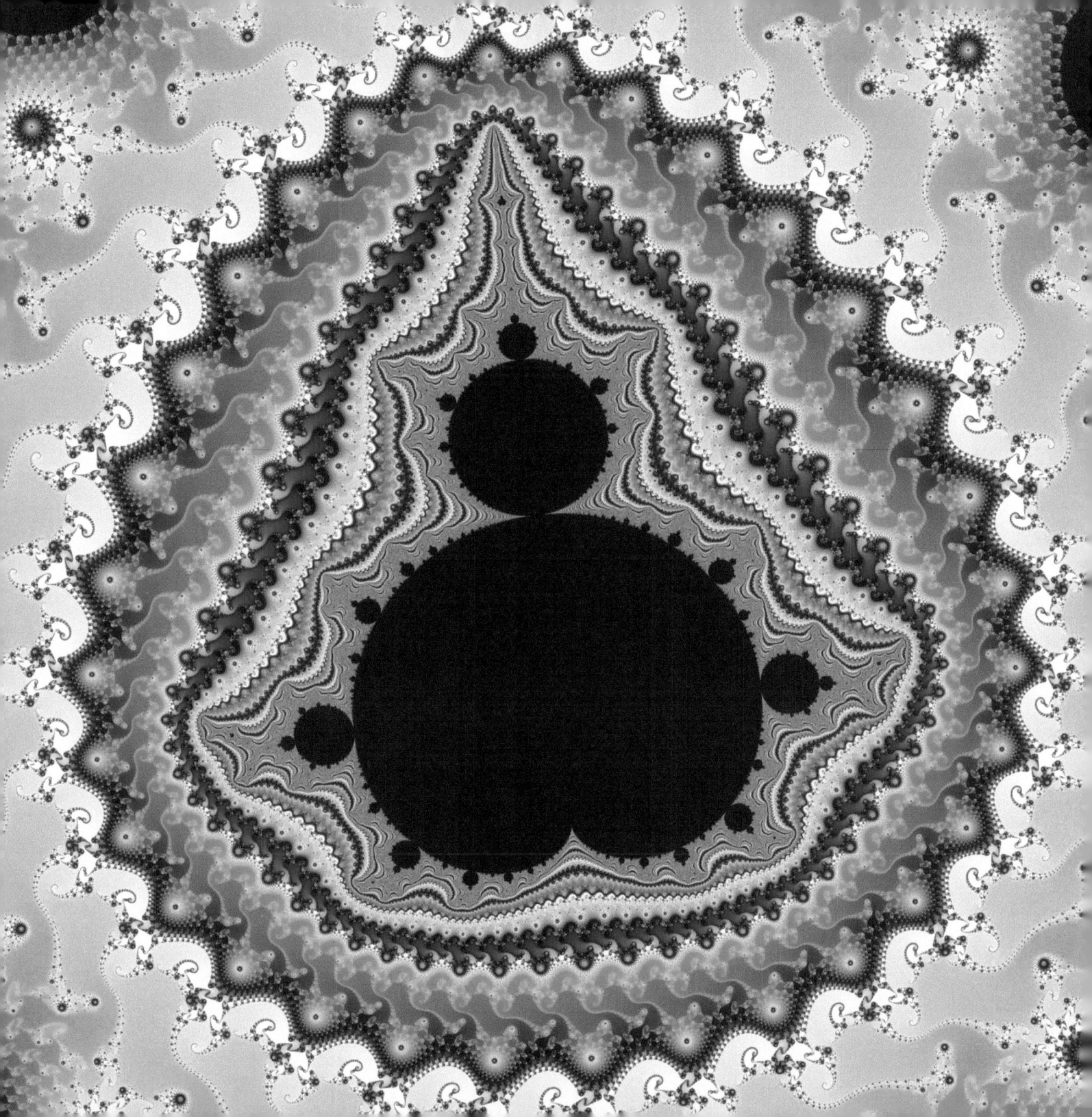

Part II

Deep field exploration

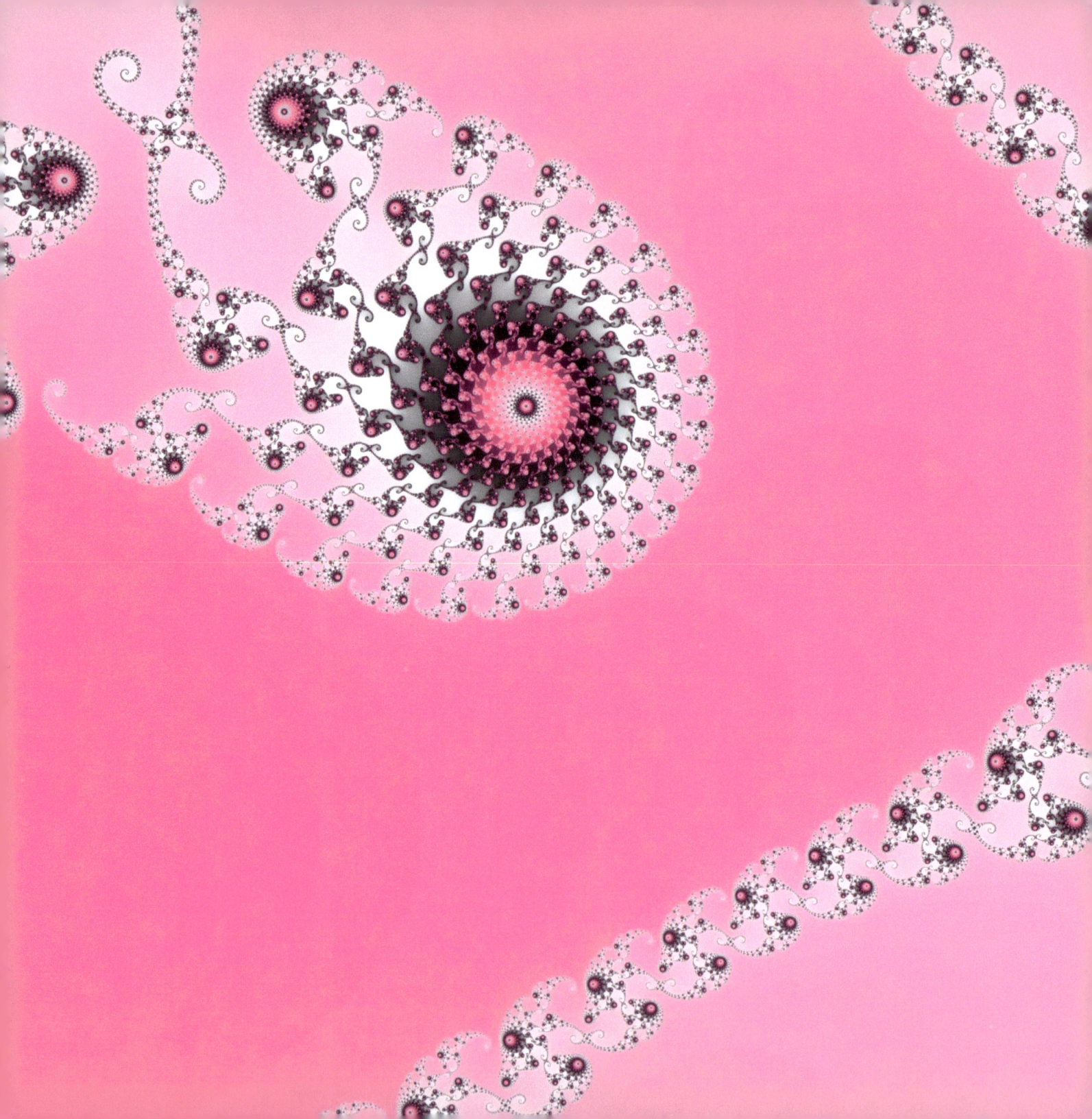

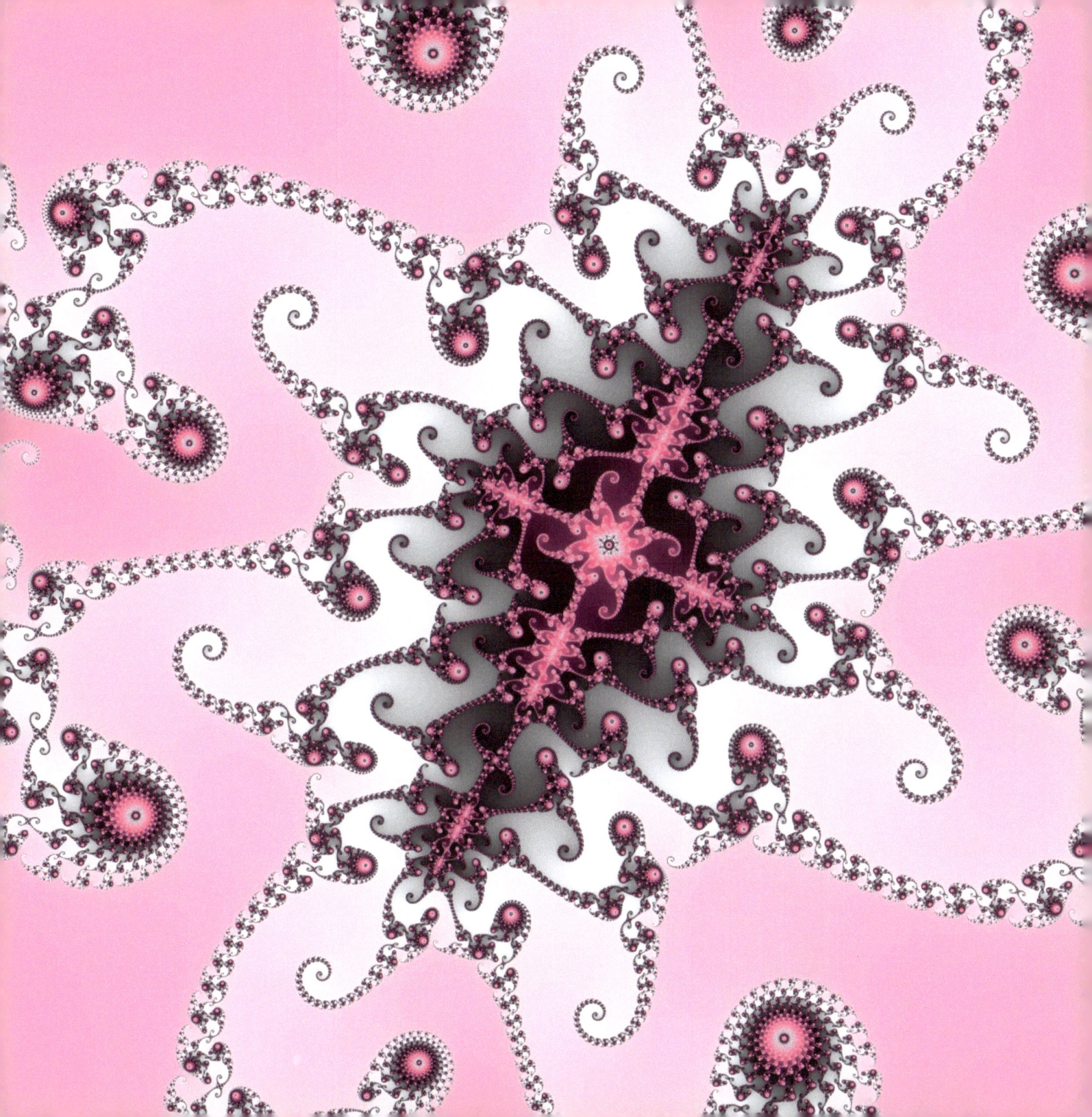

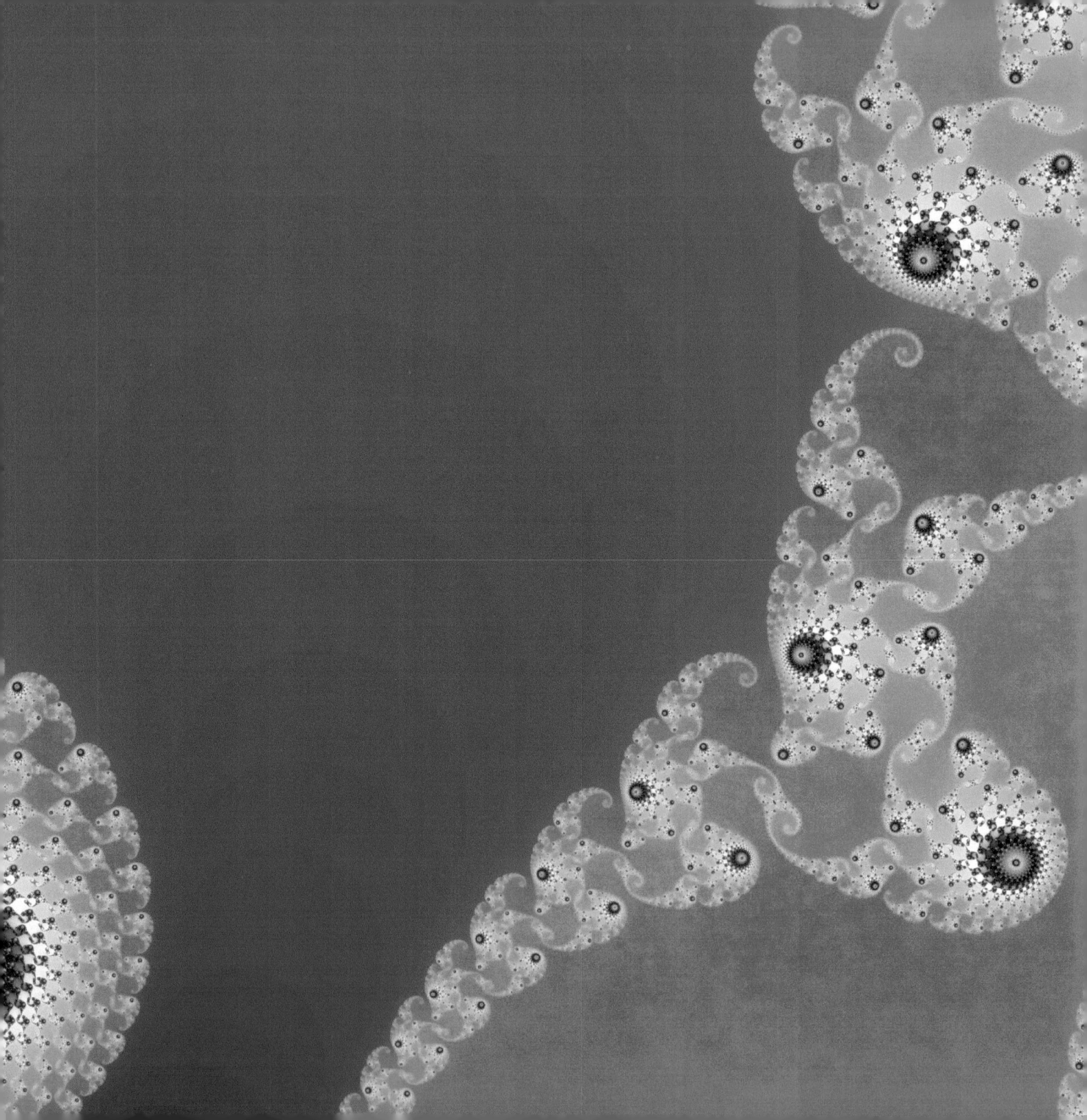

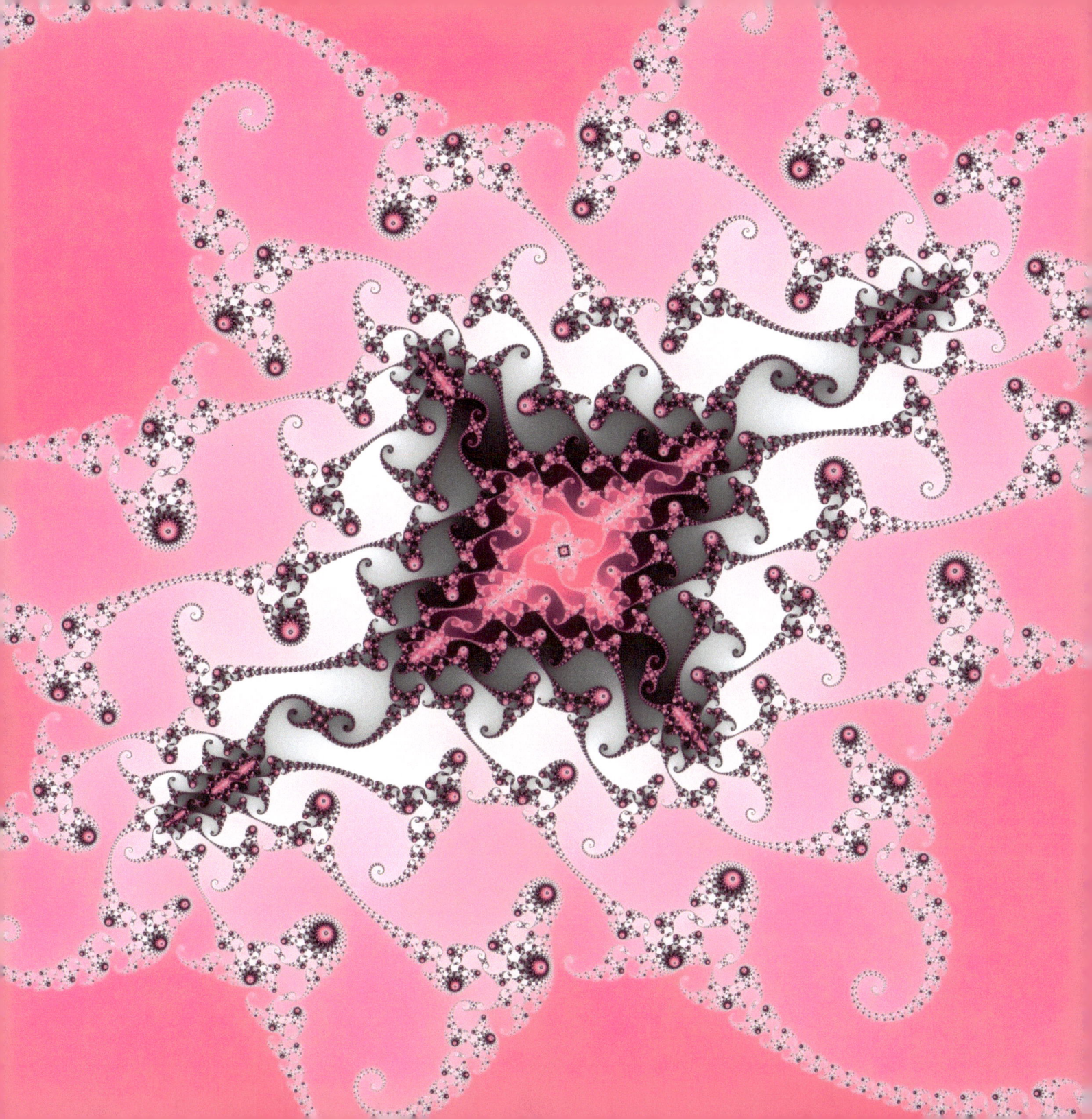

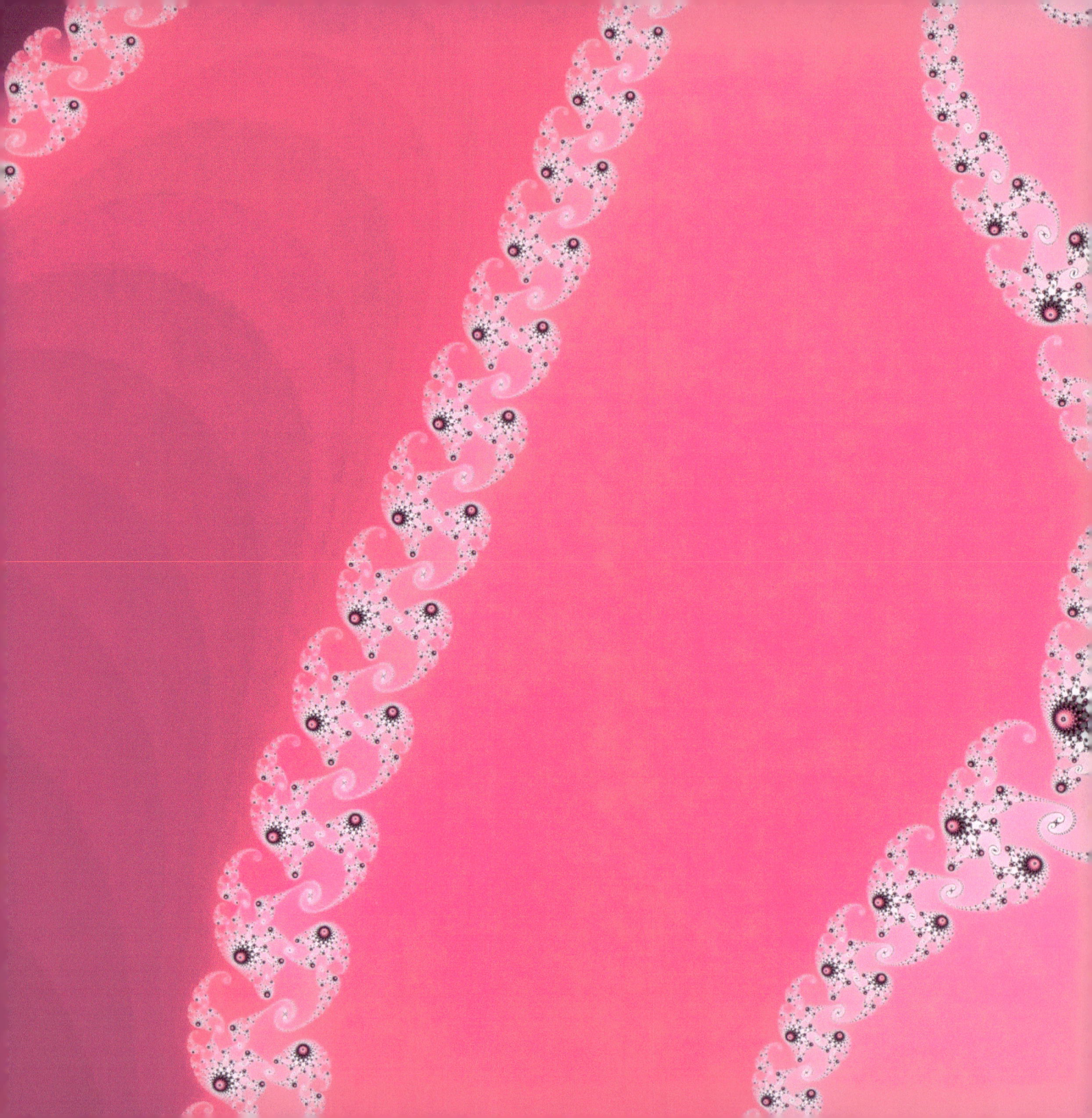

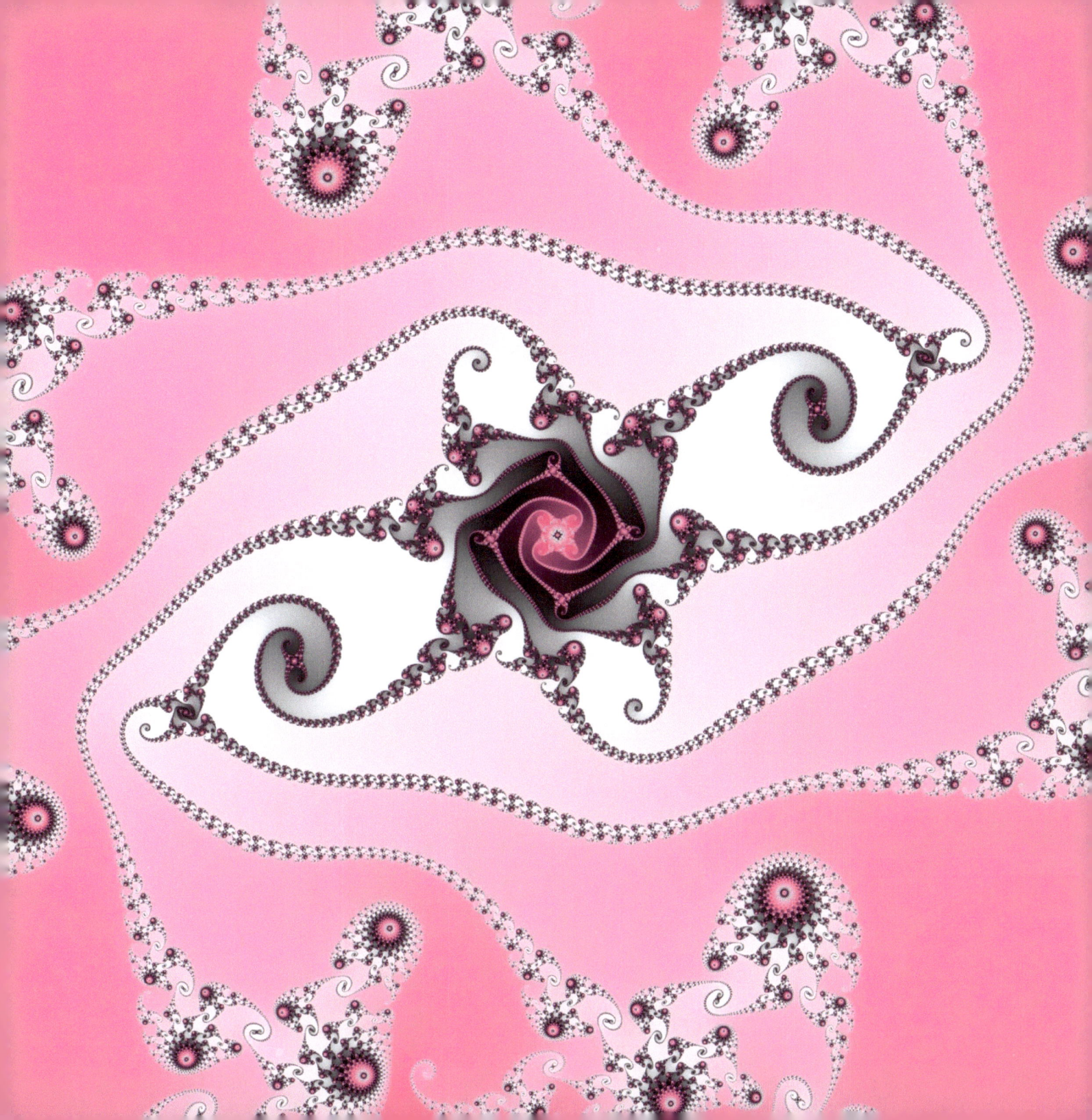

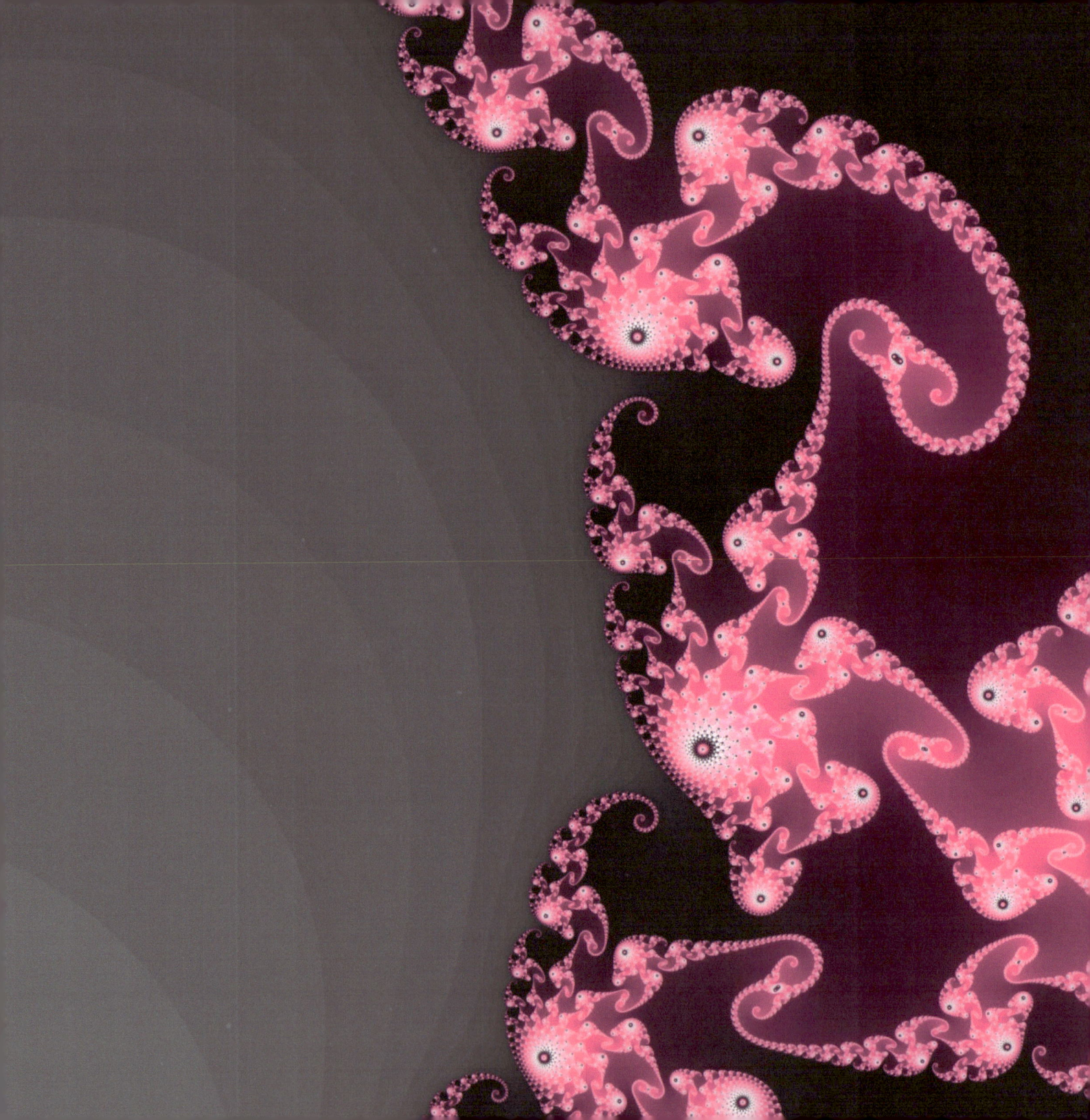

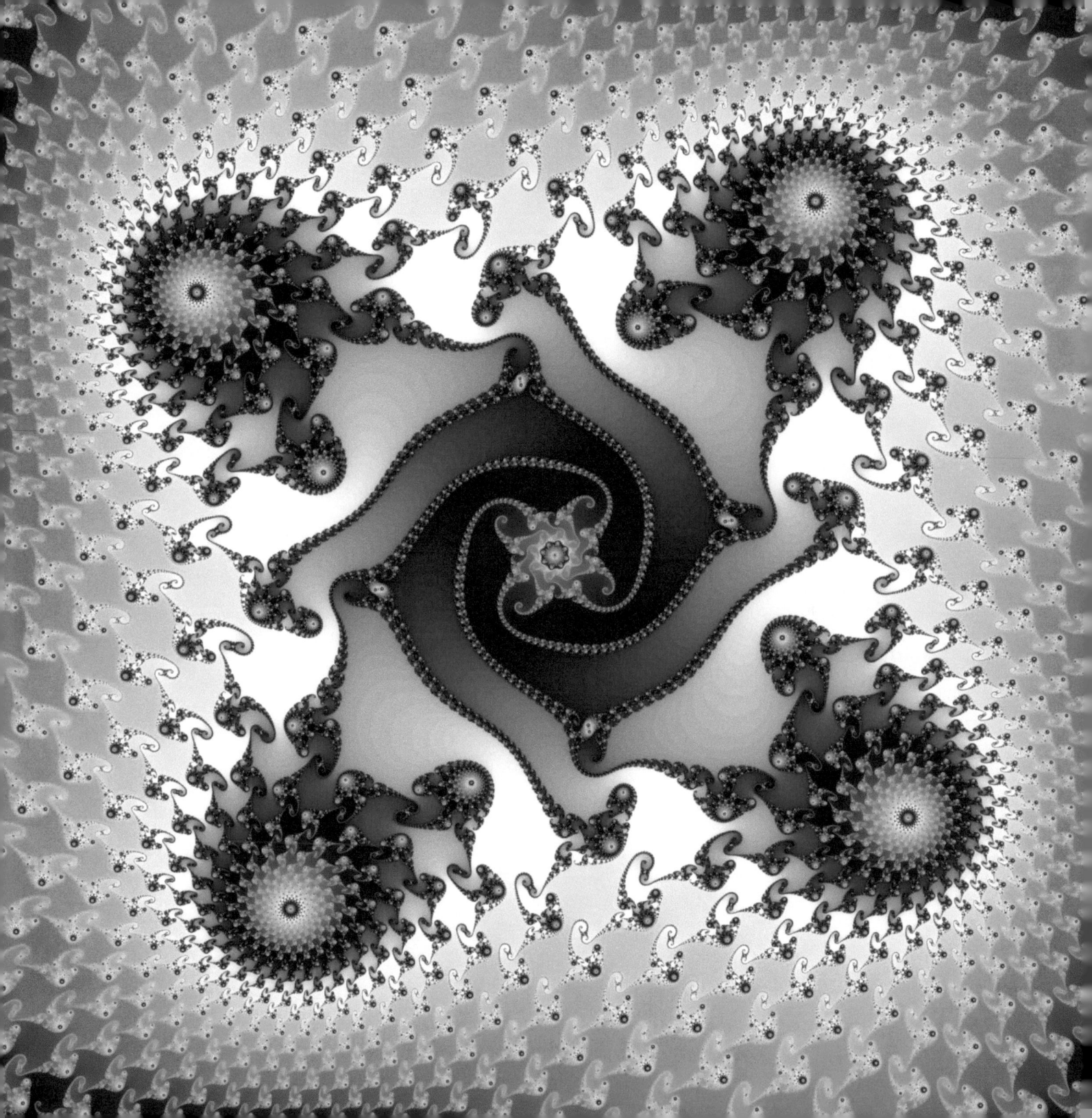

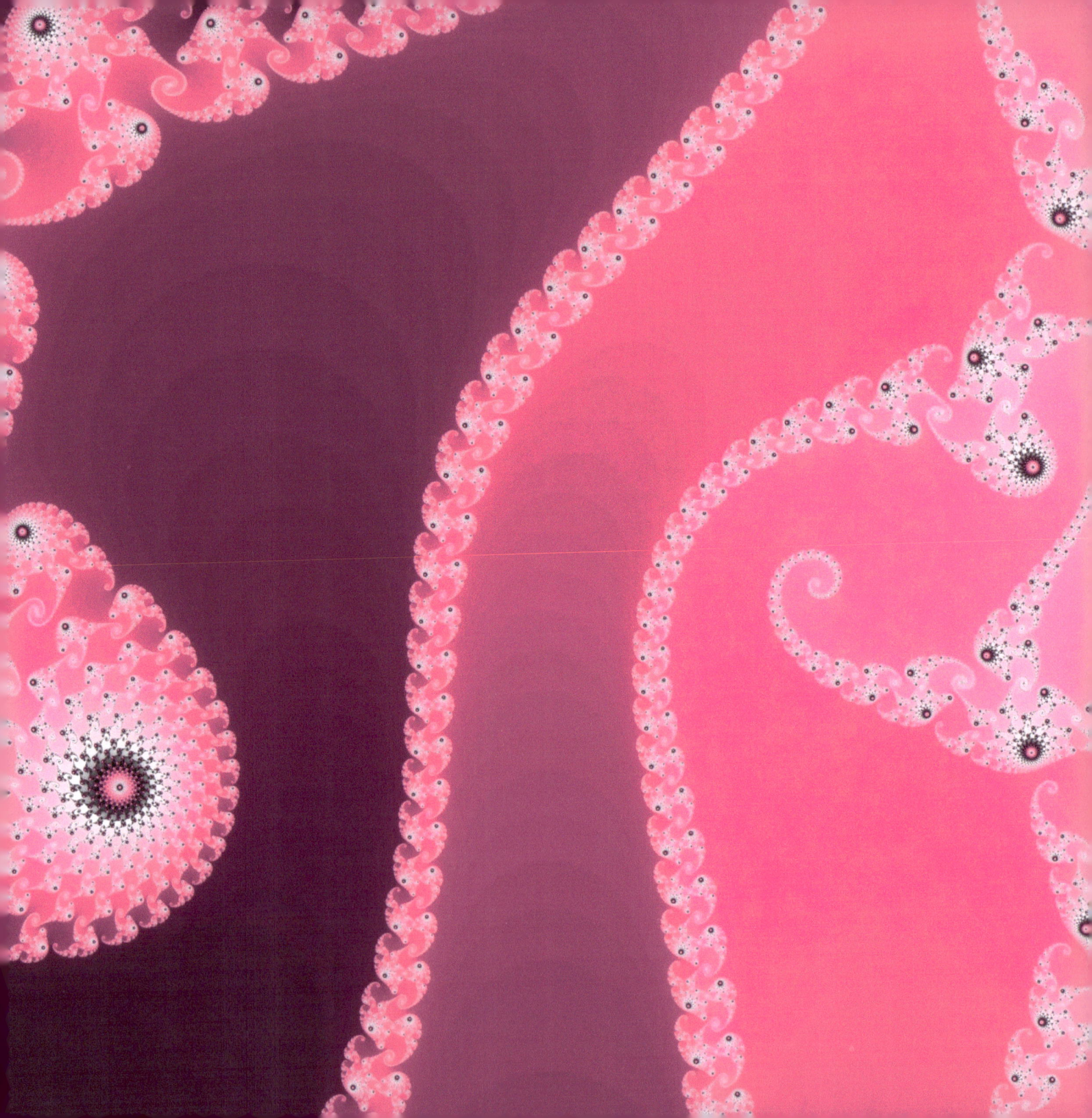

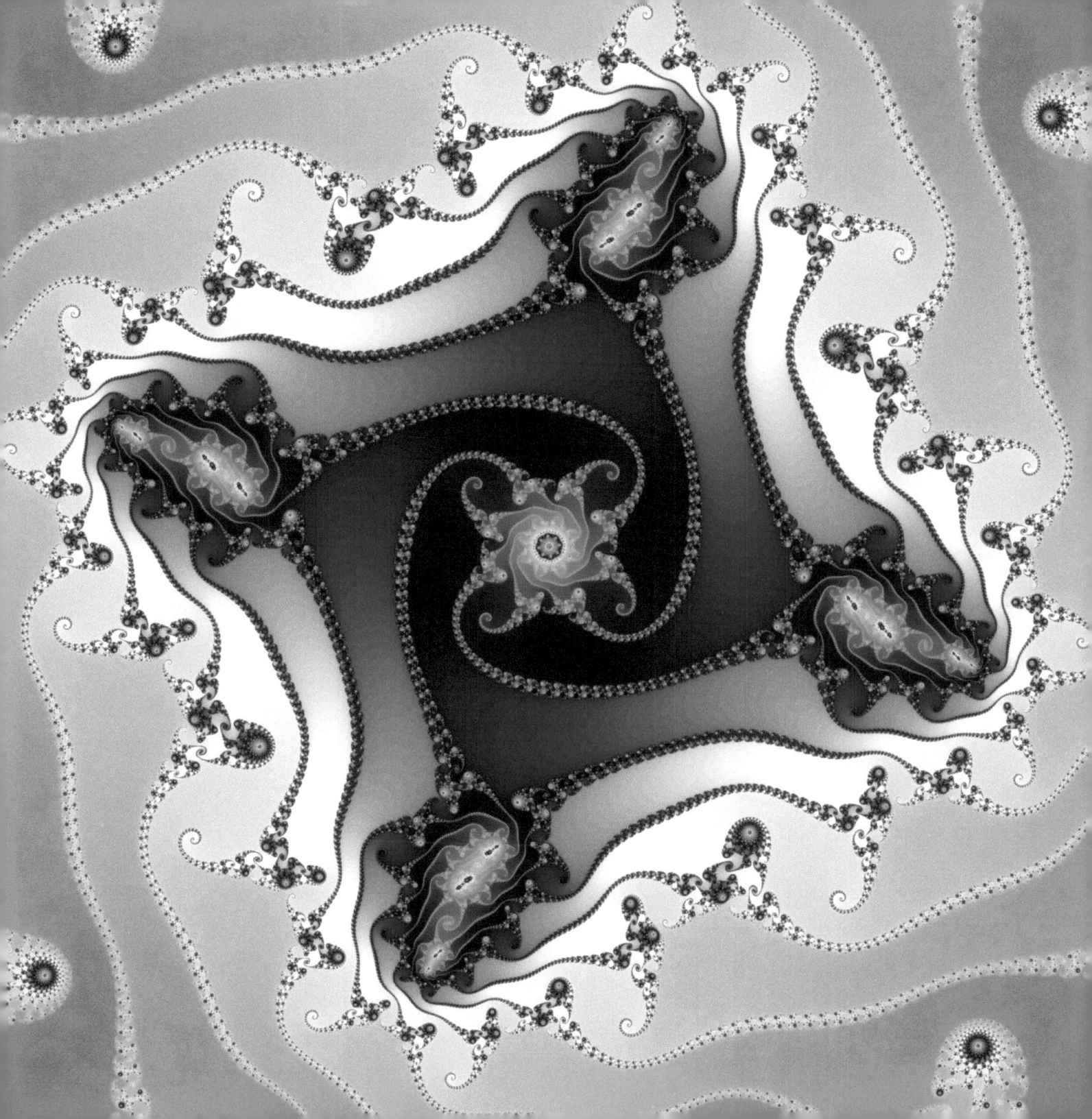

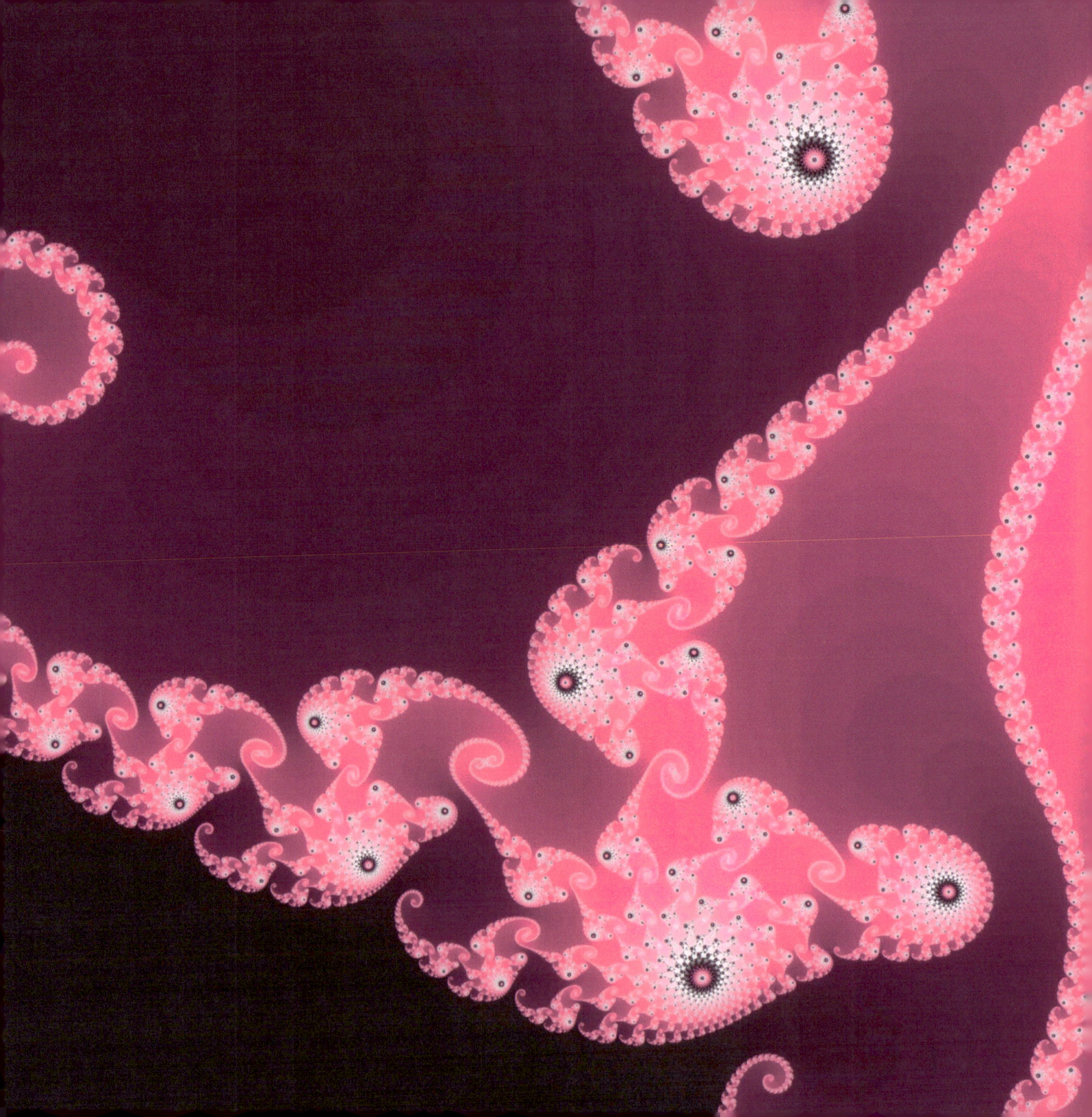

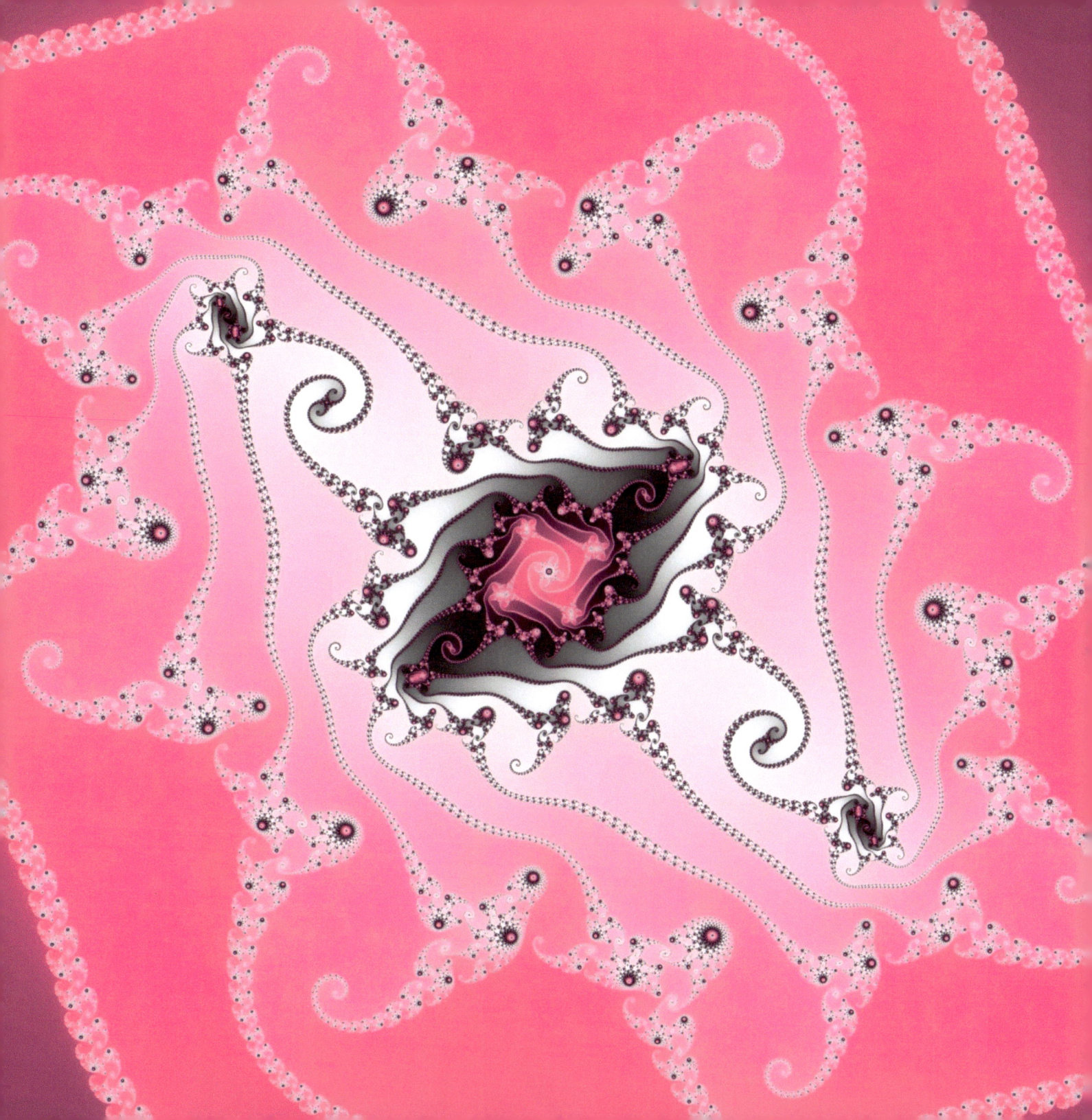

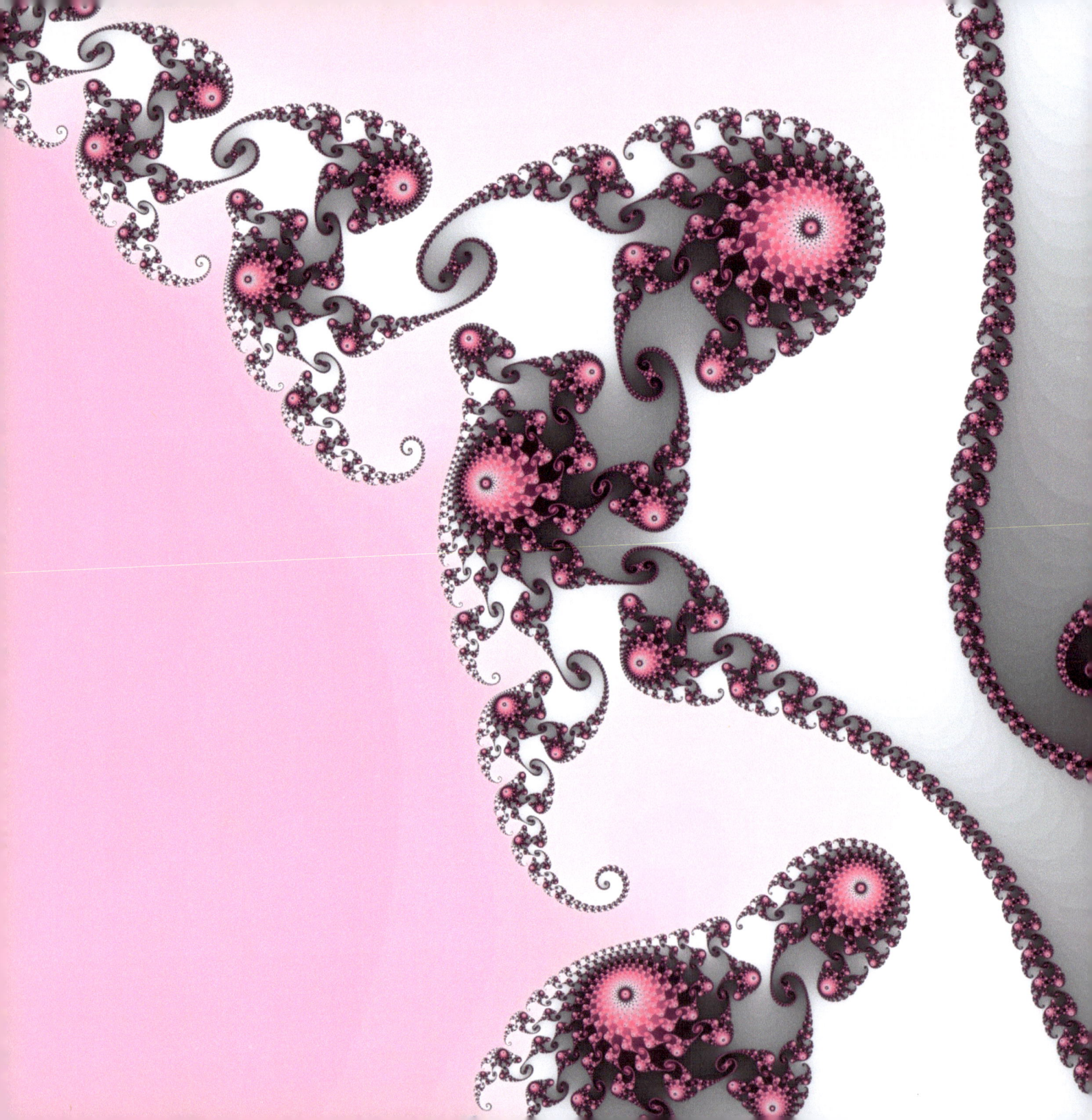

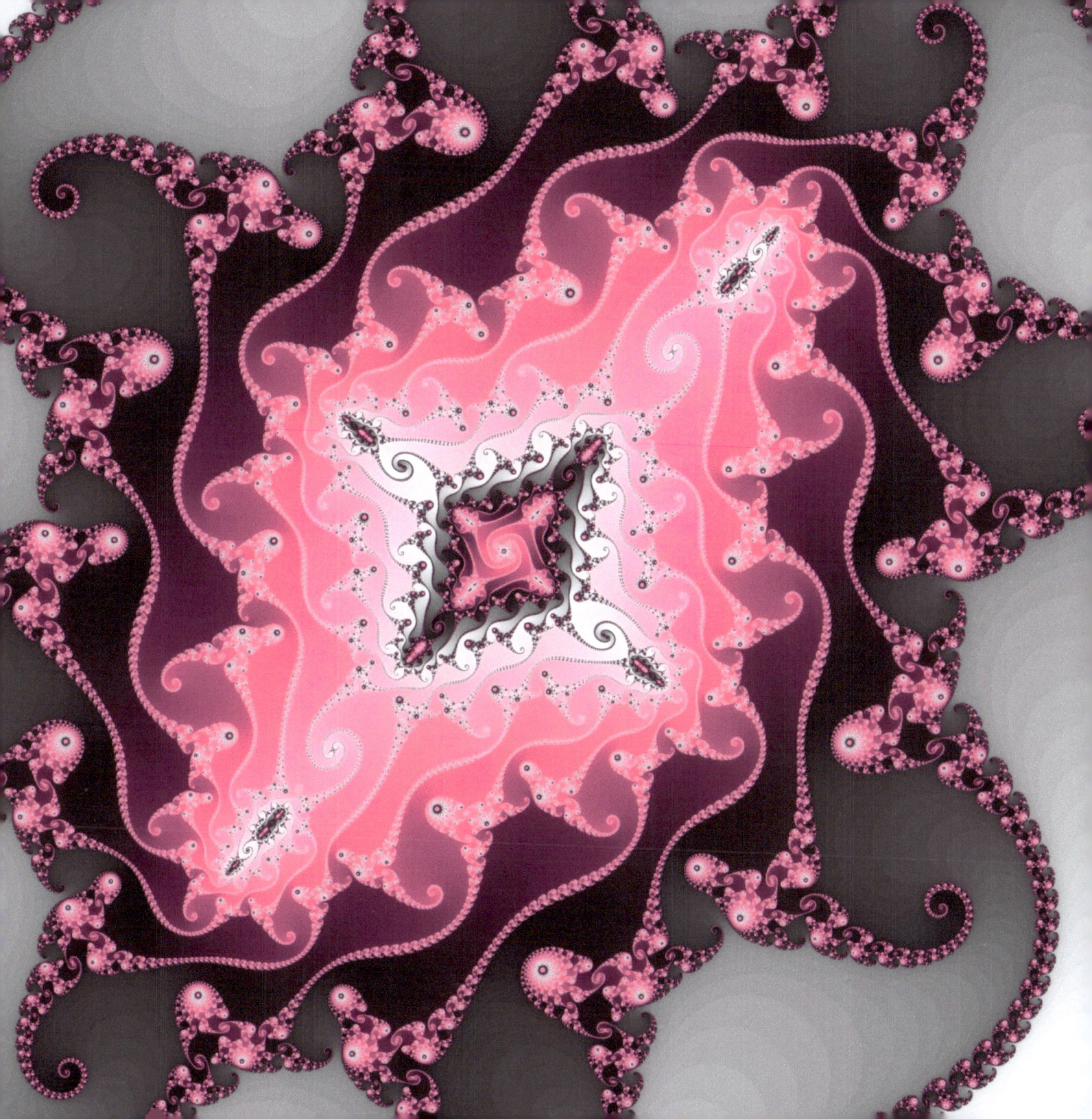

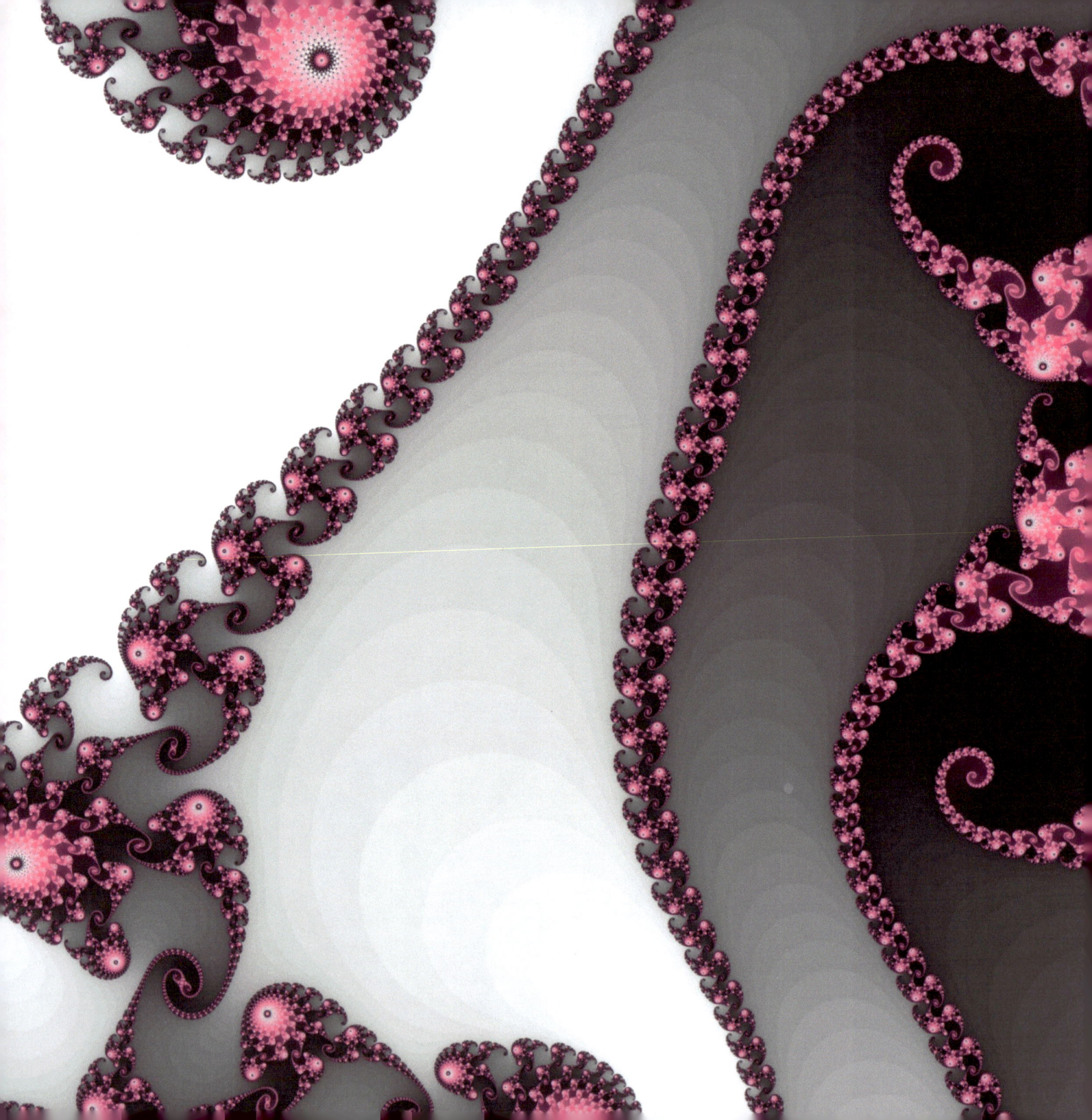

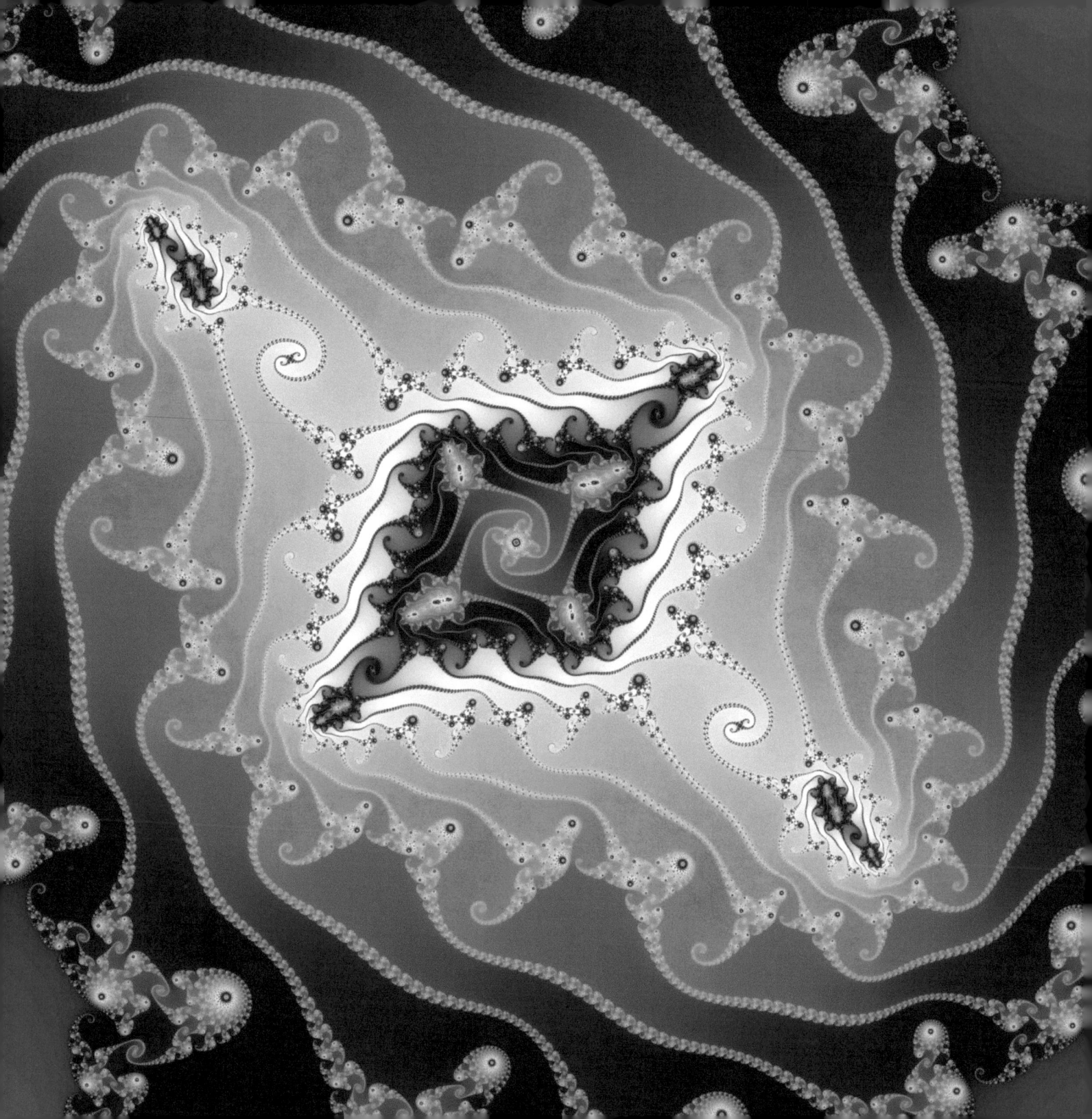

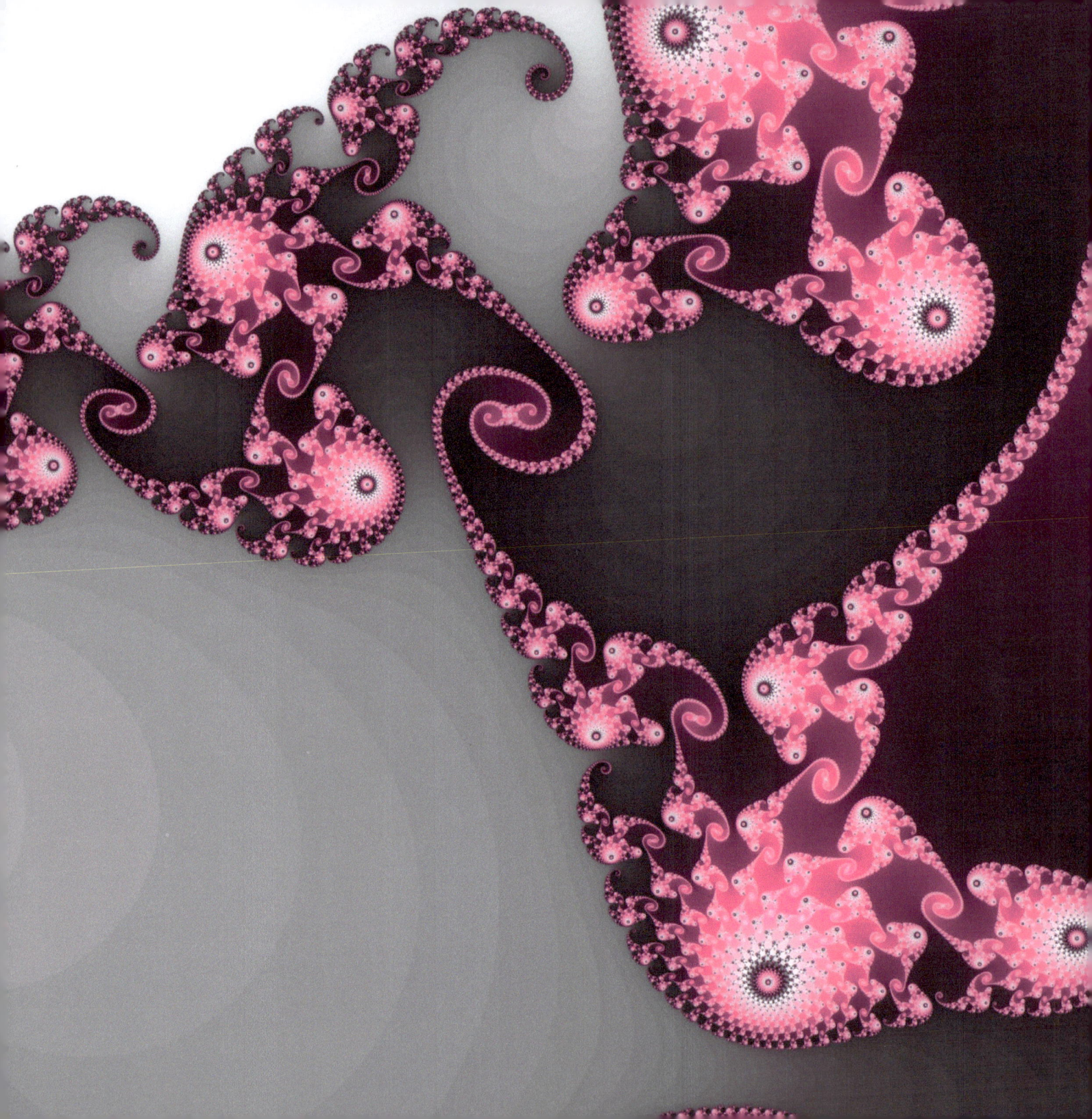

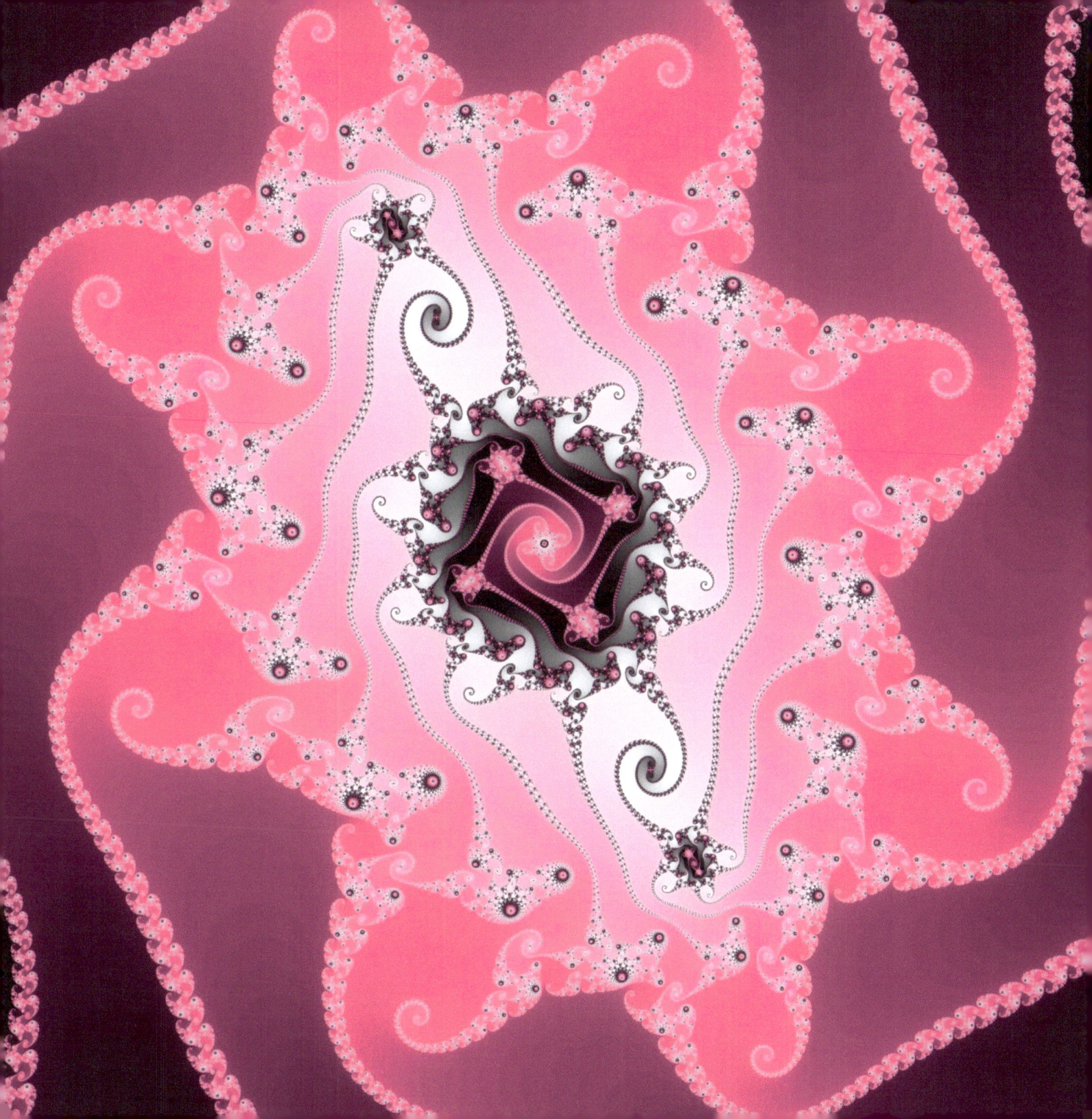

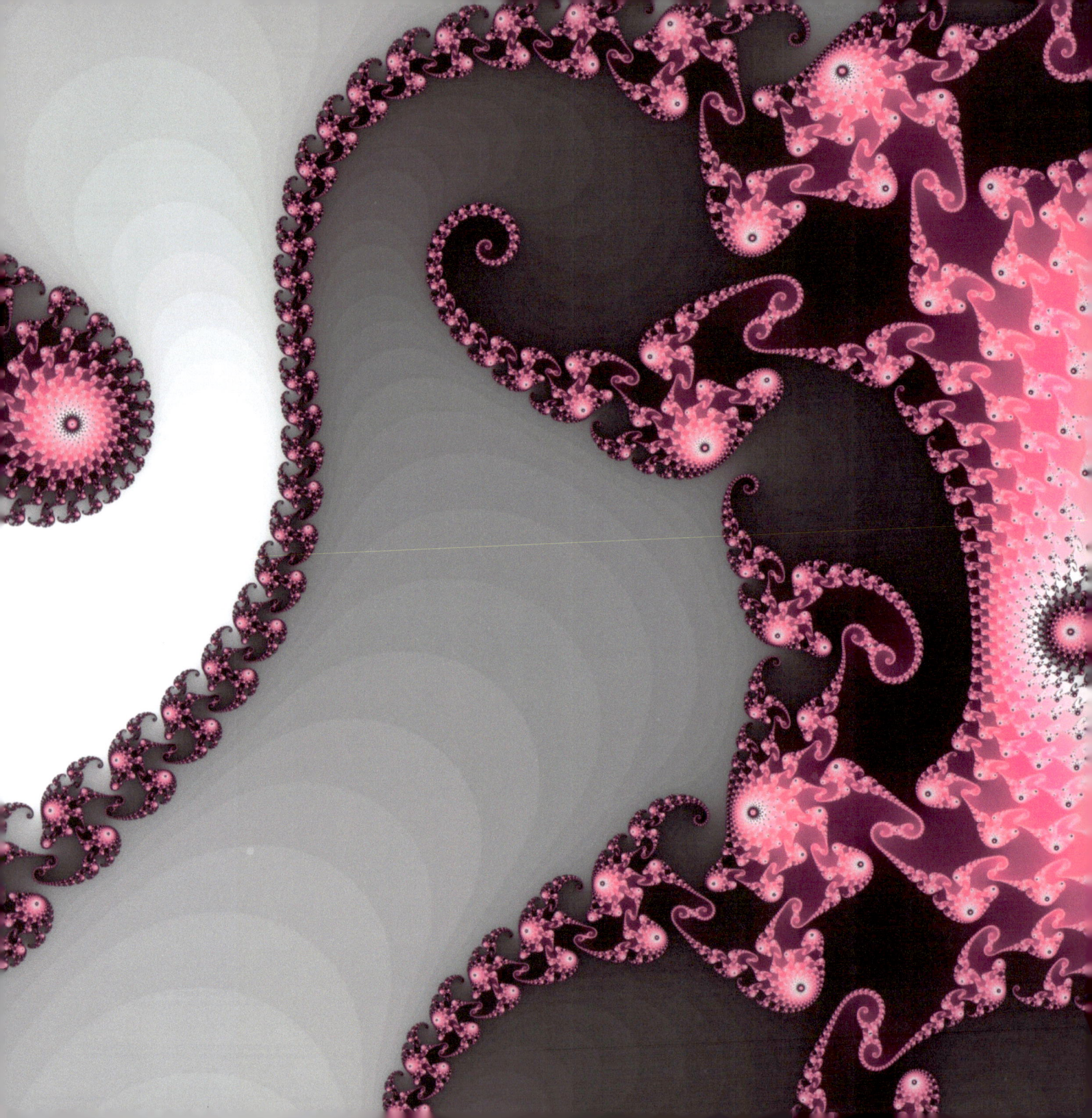

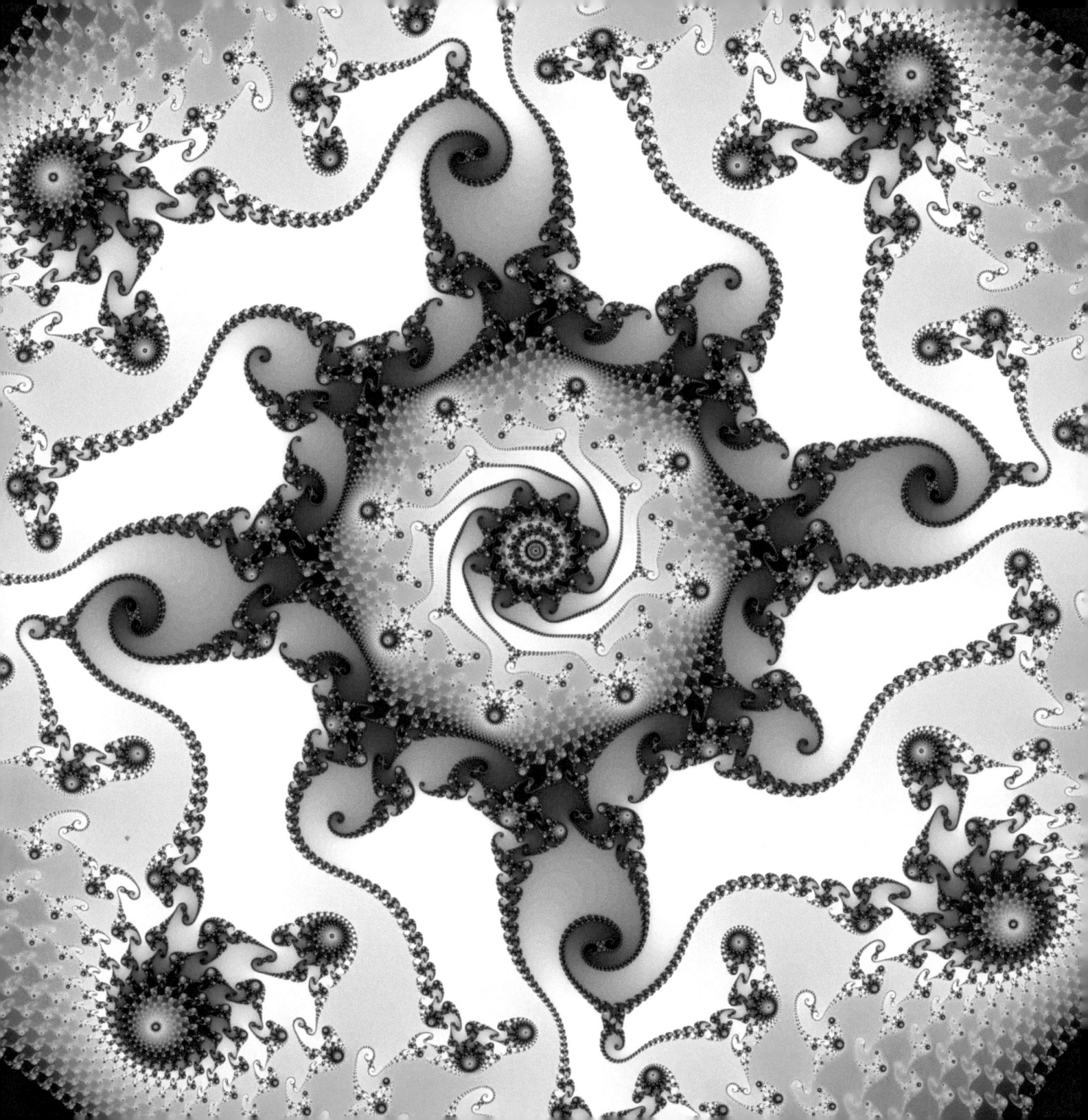

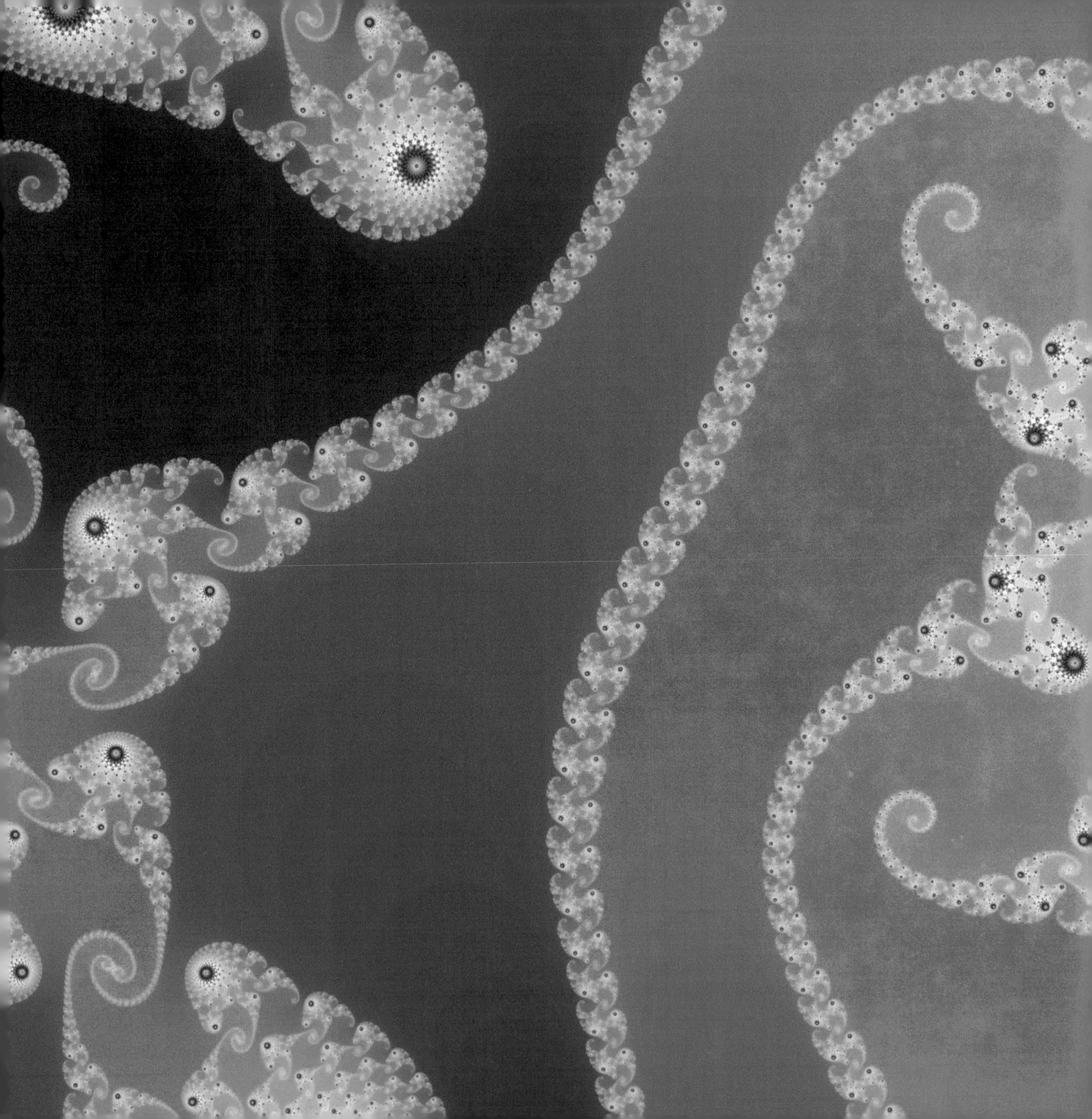

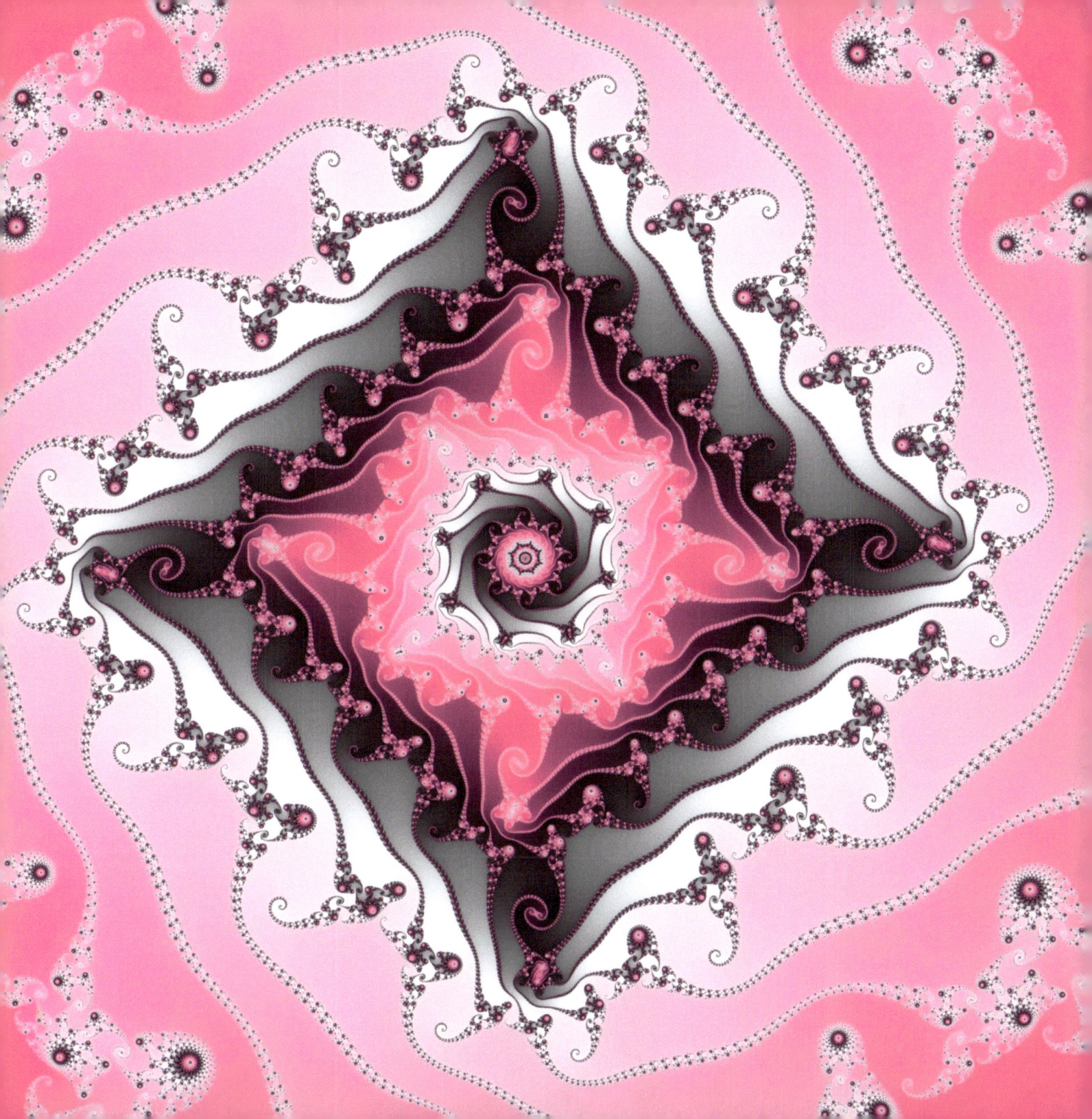

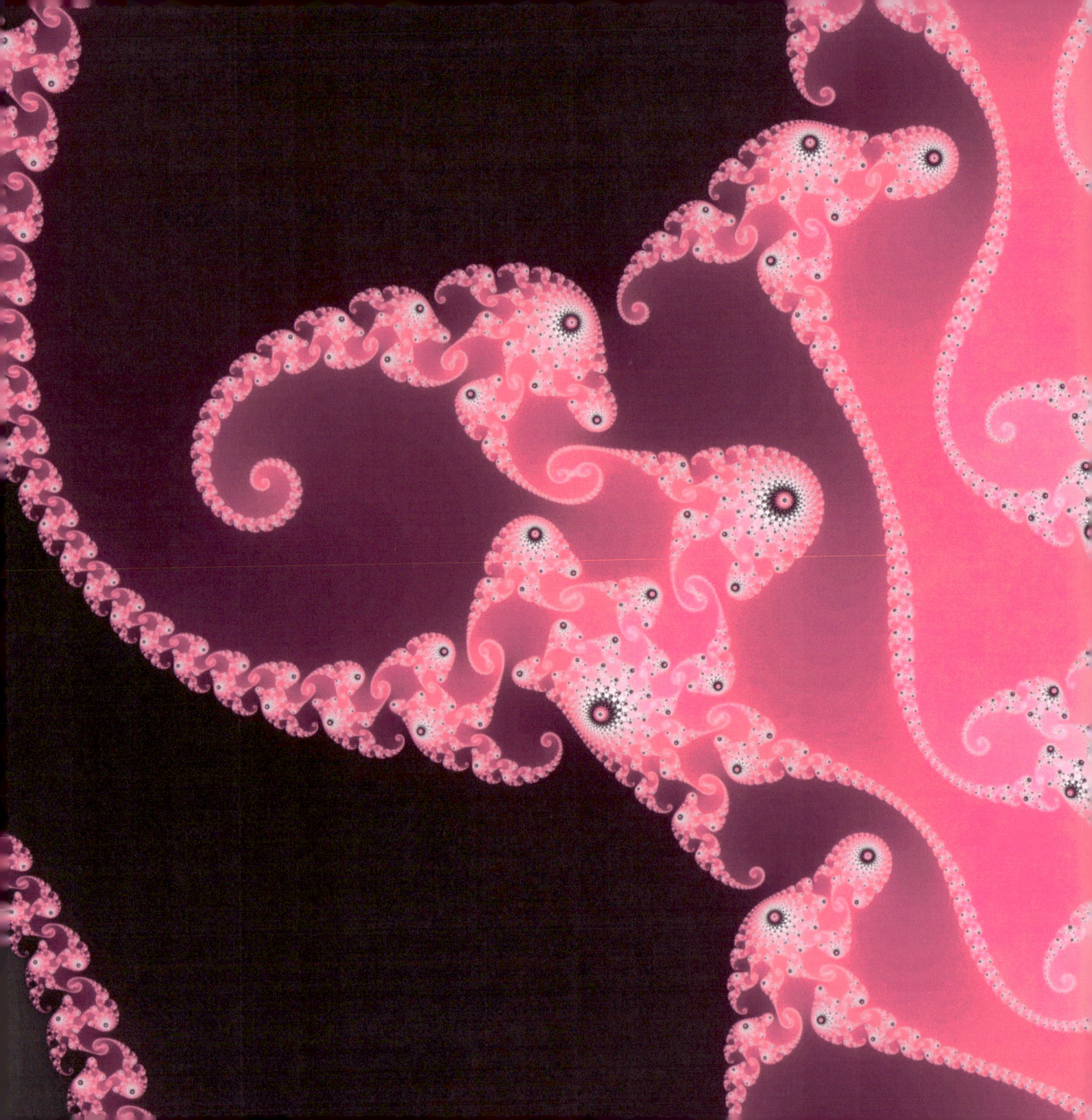

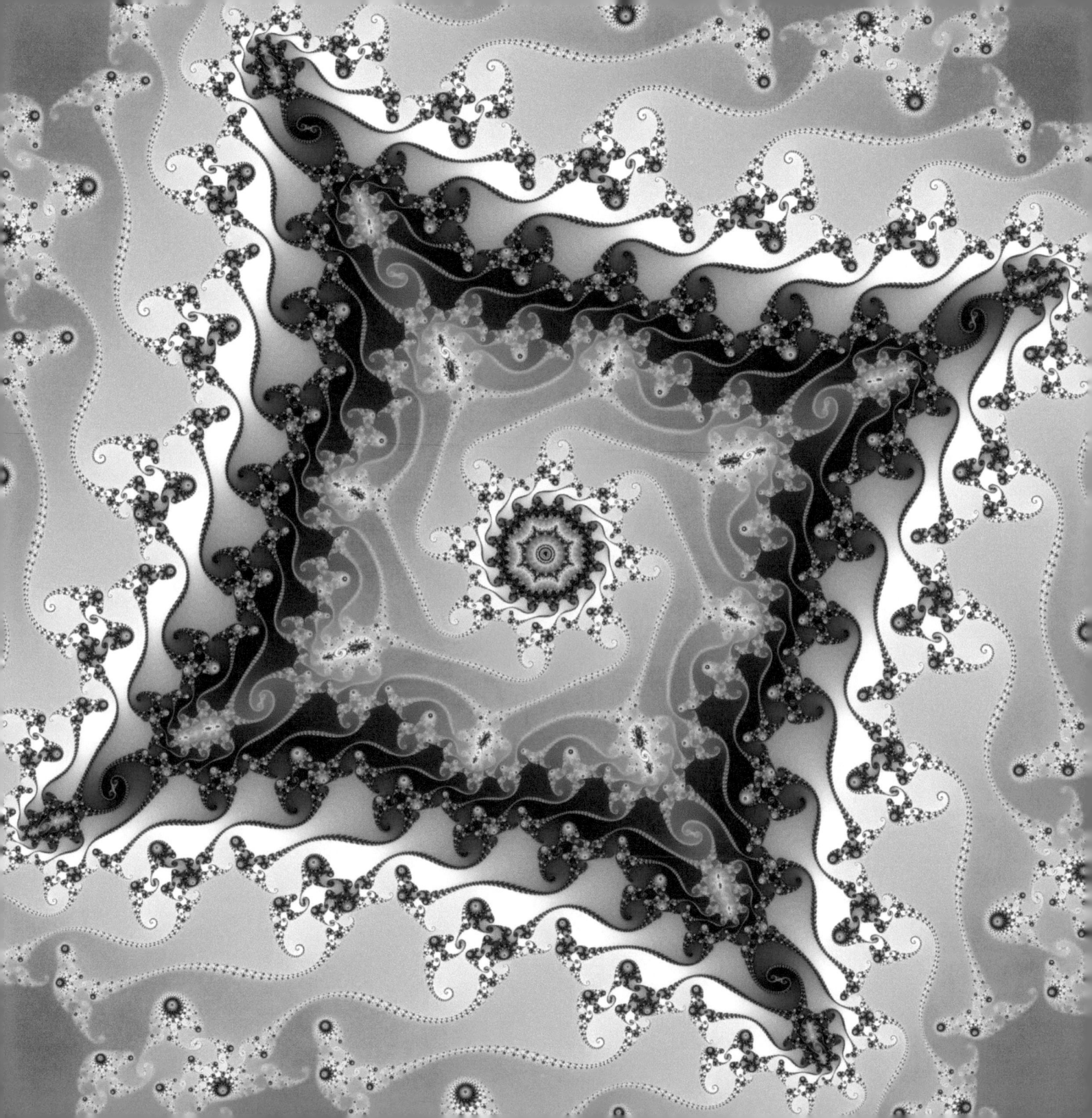

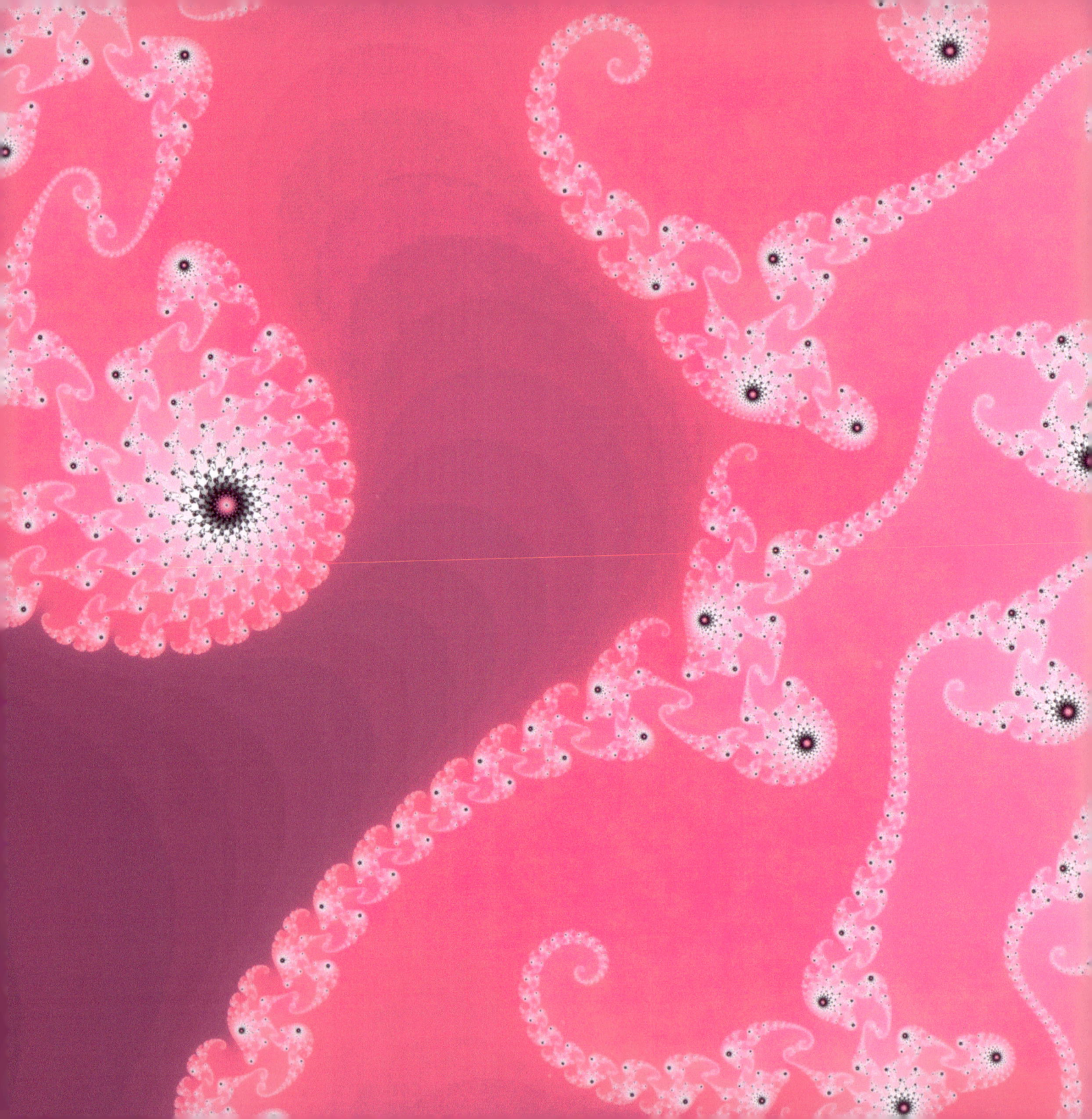

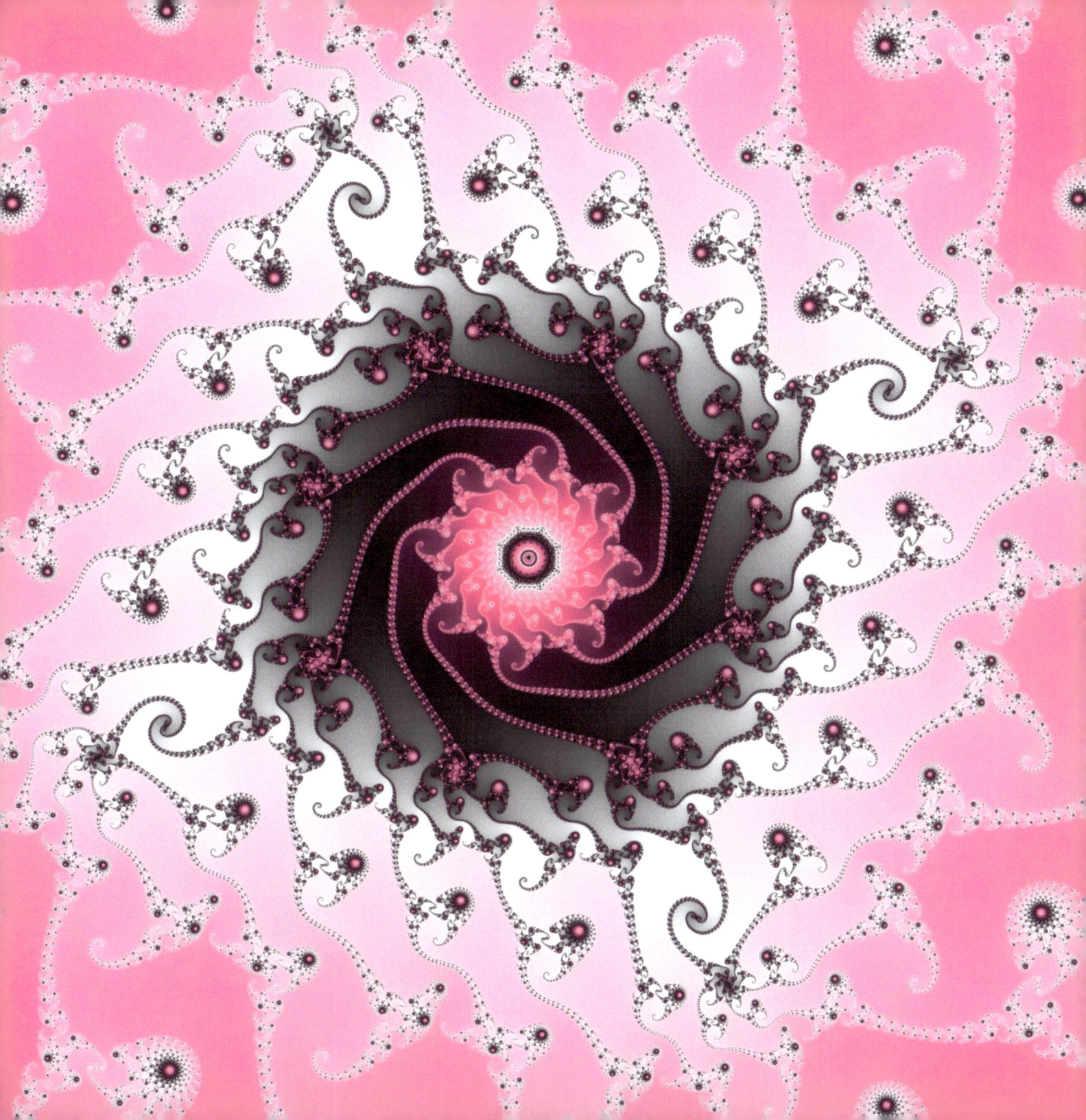

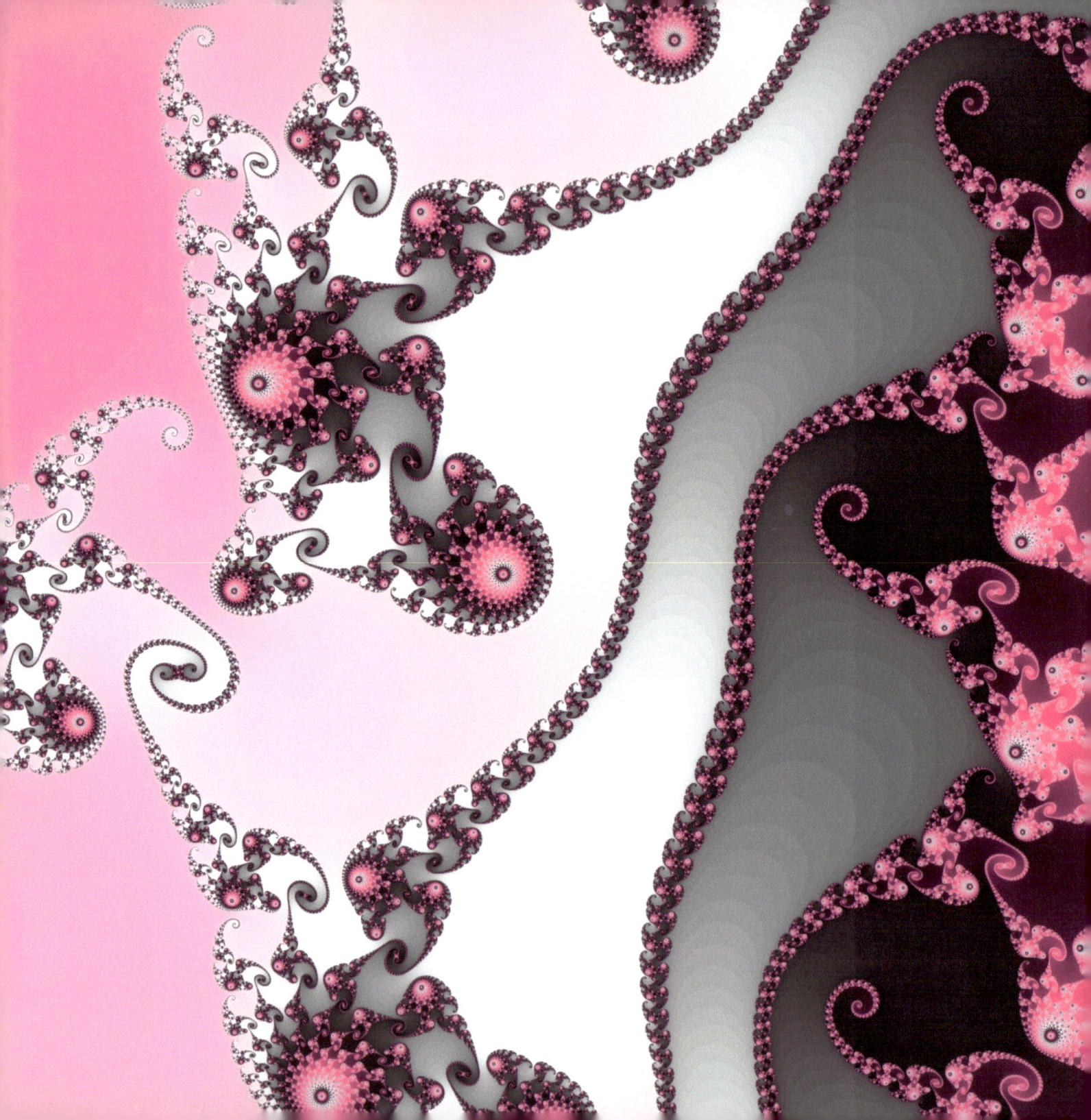

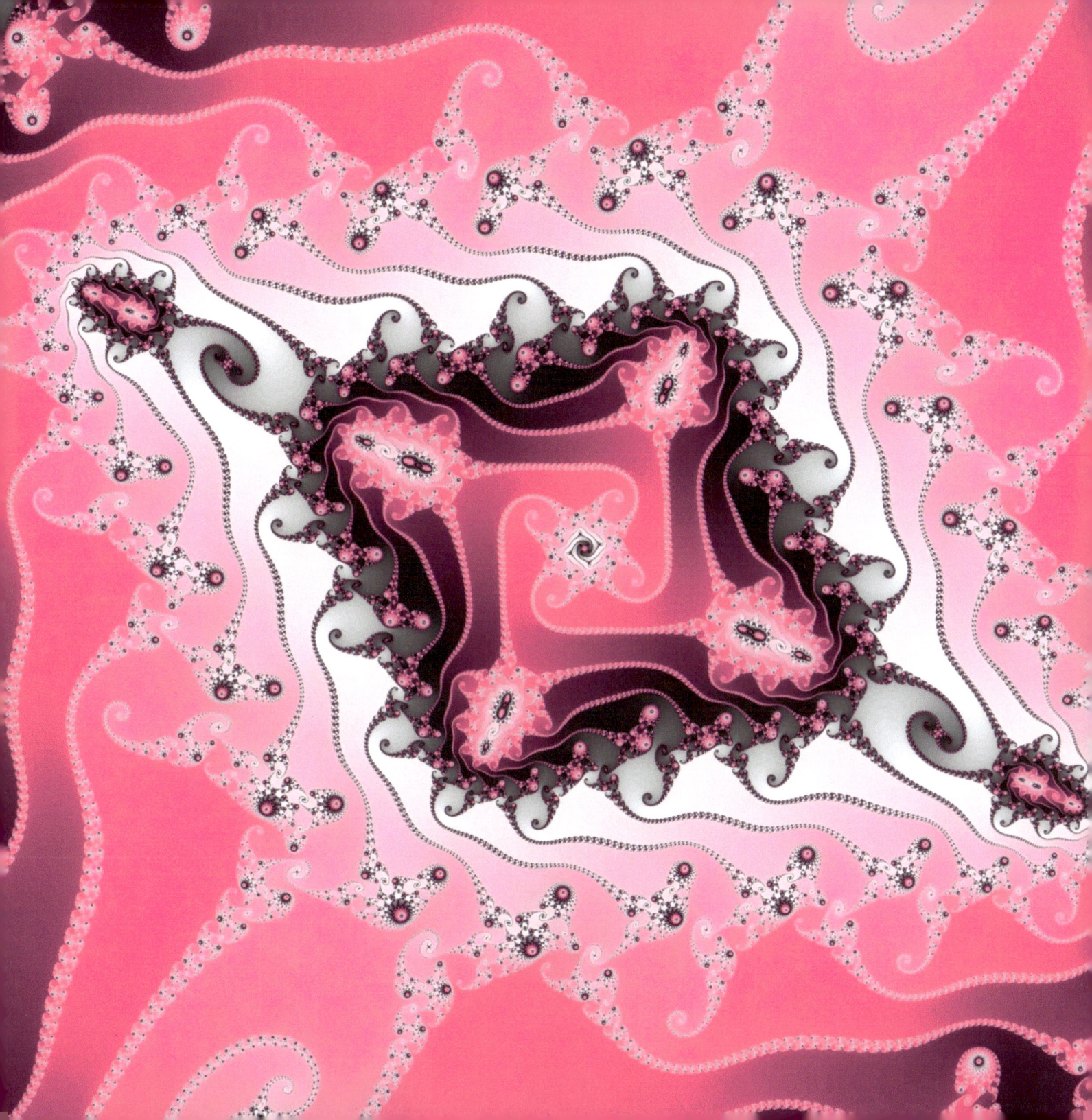

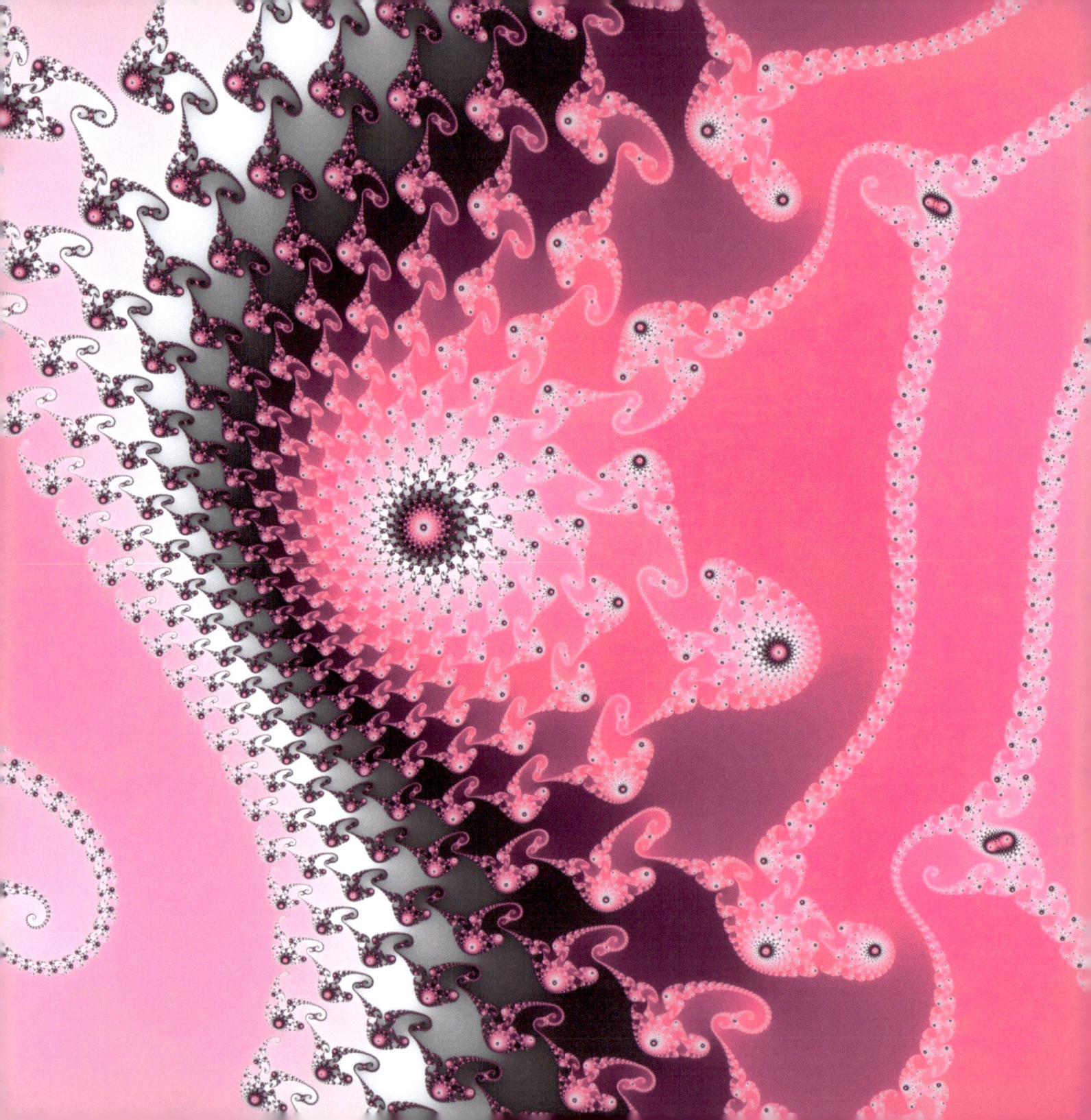

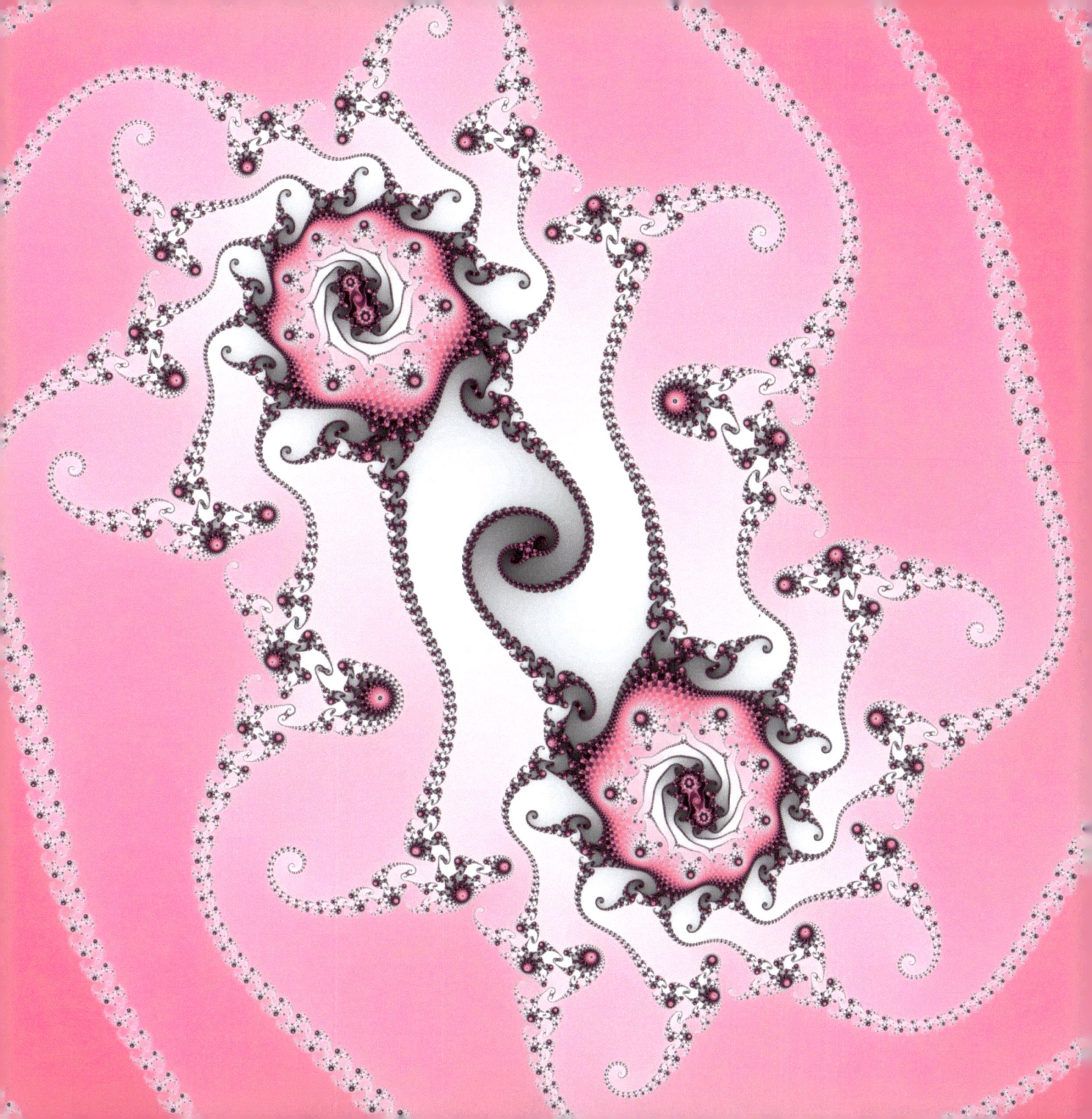

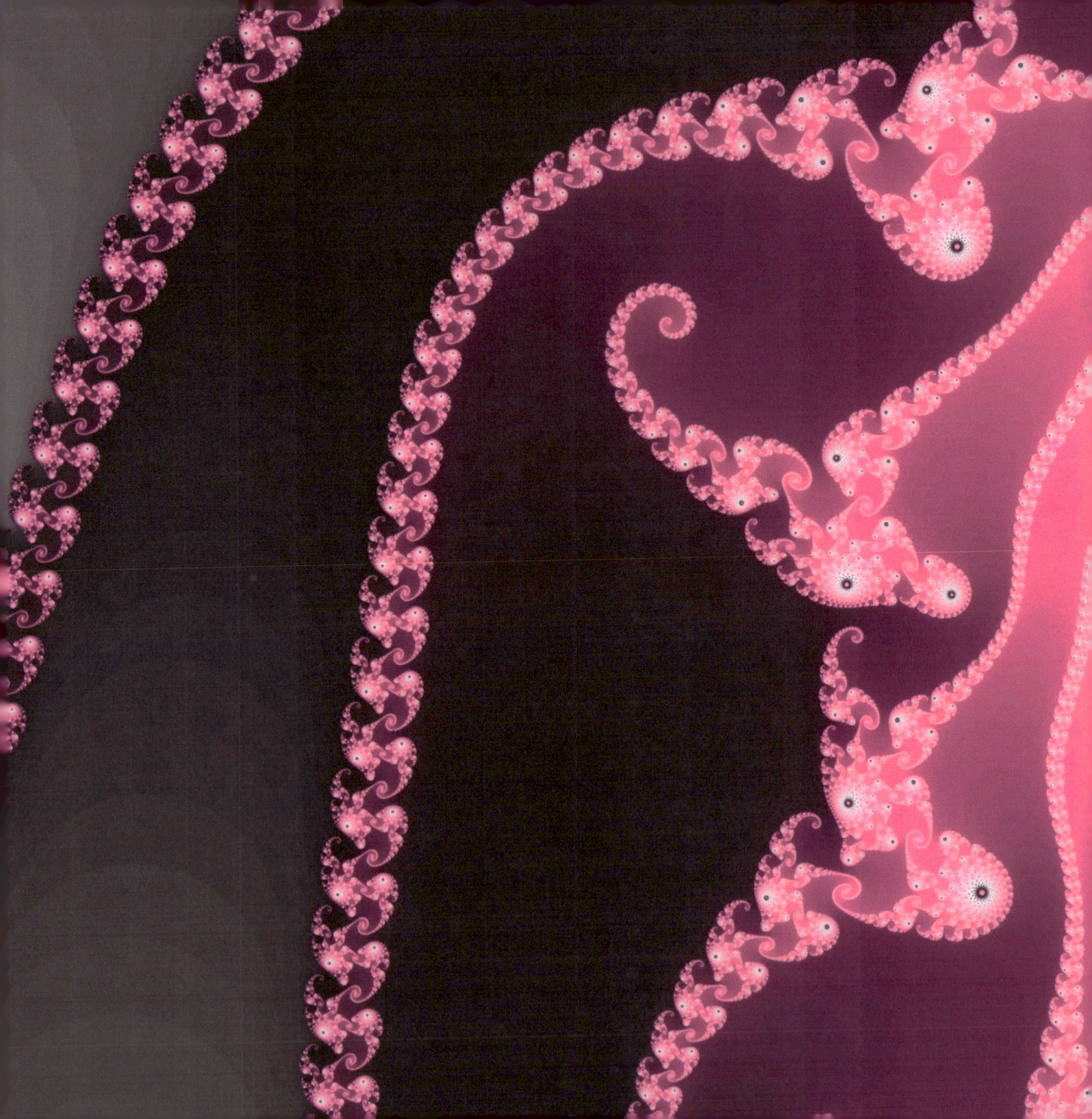

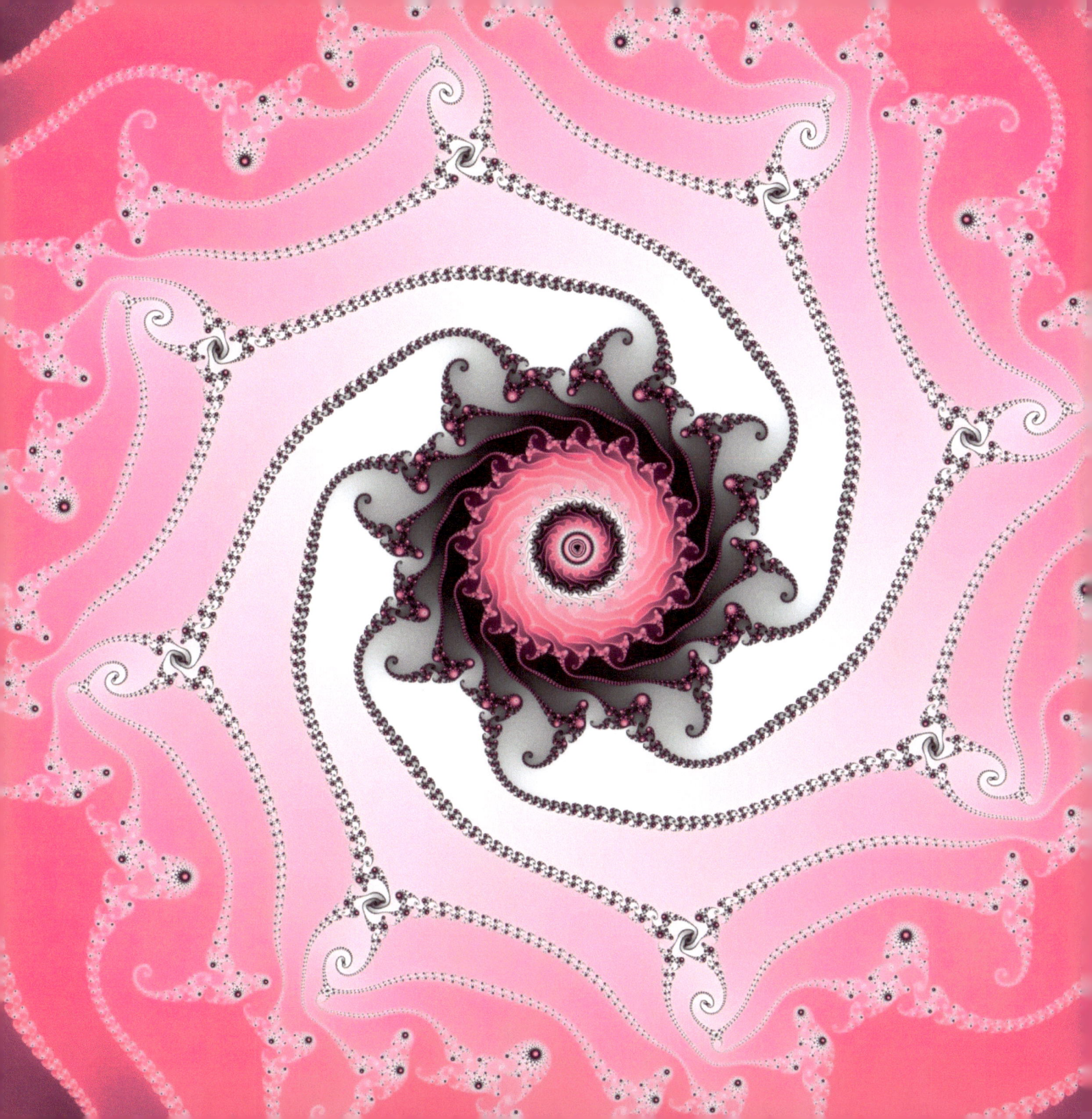

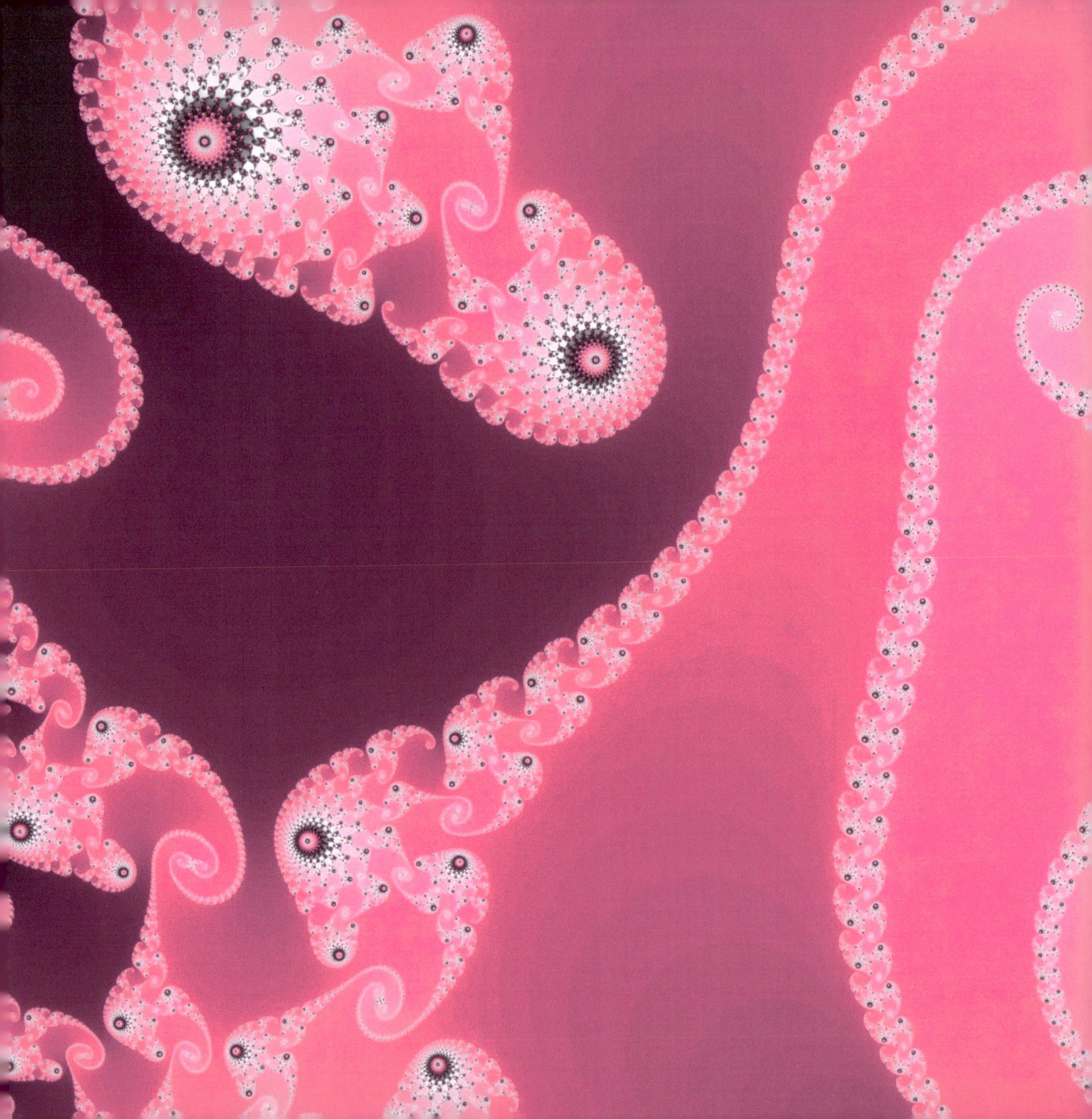

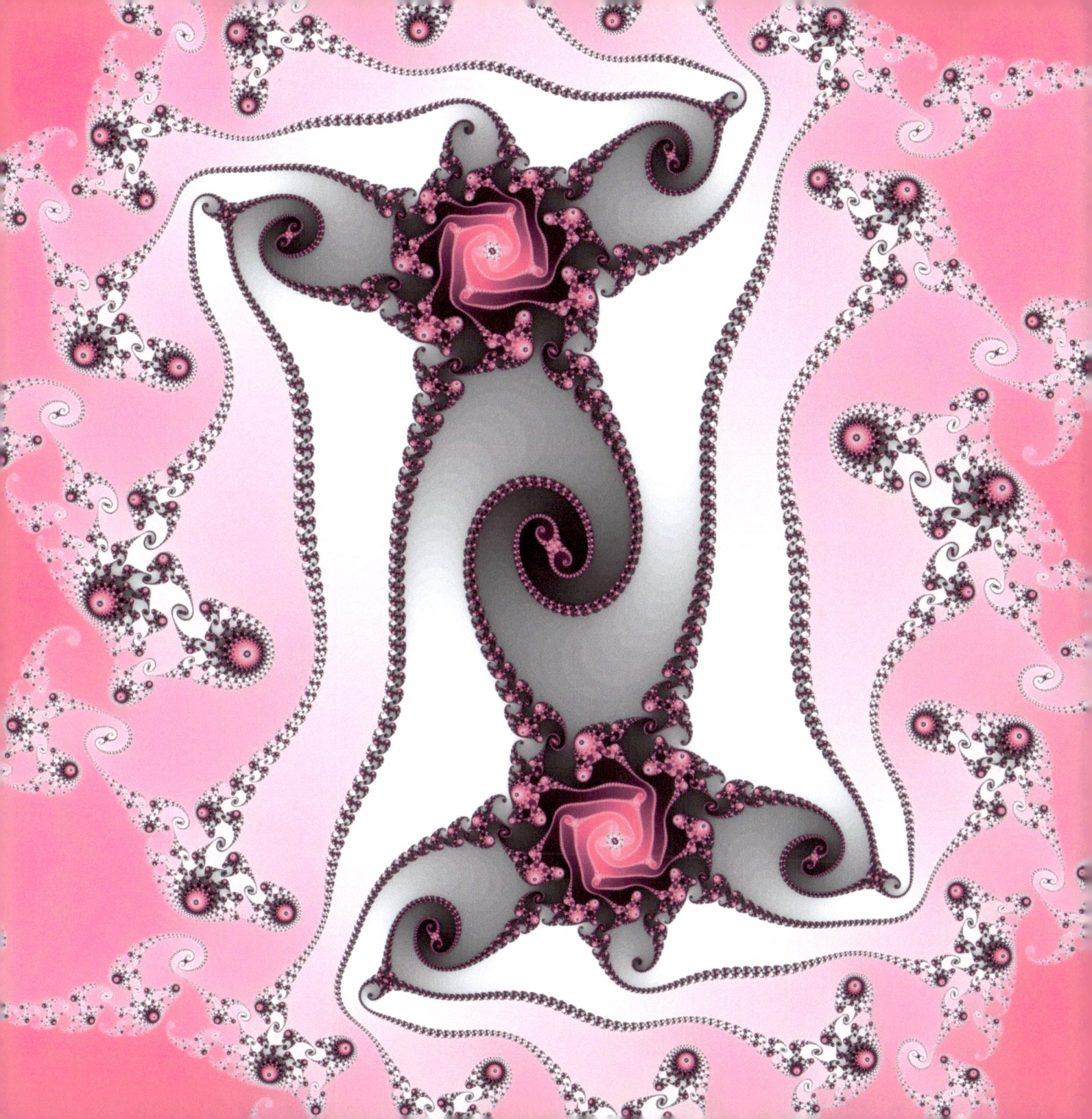

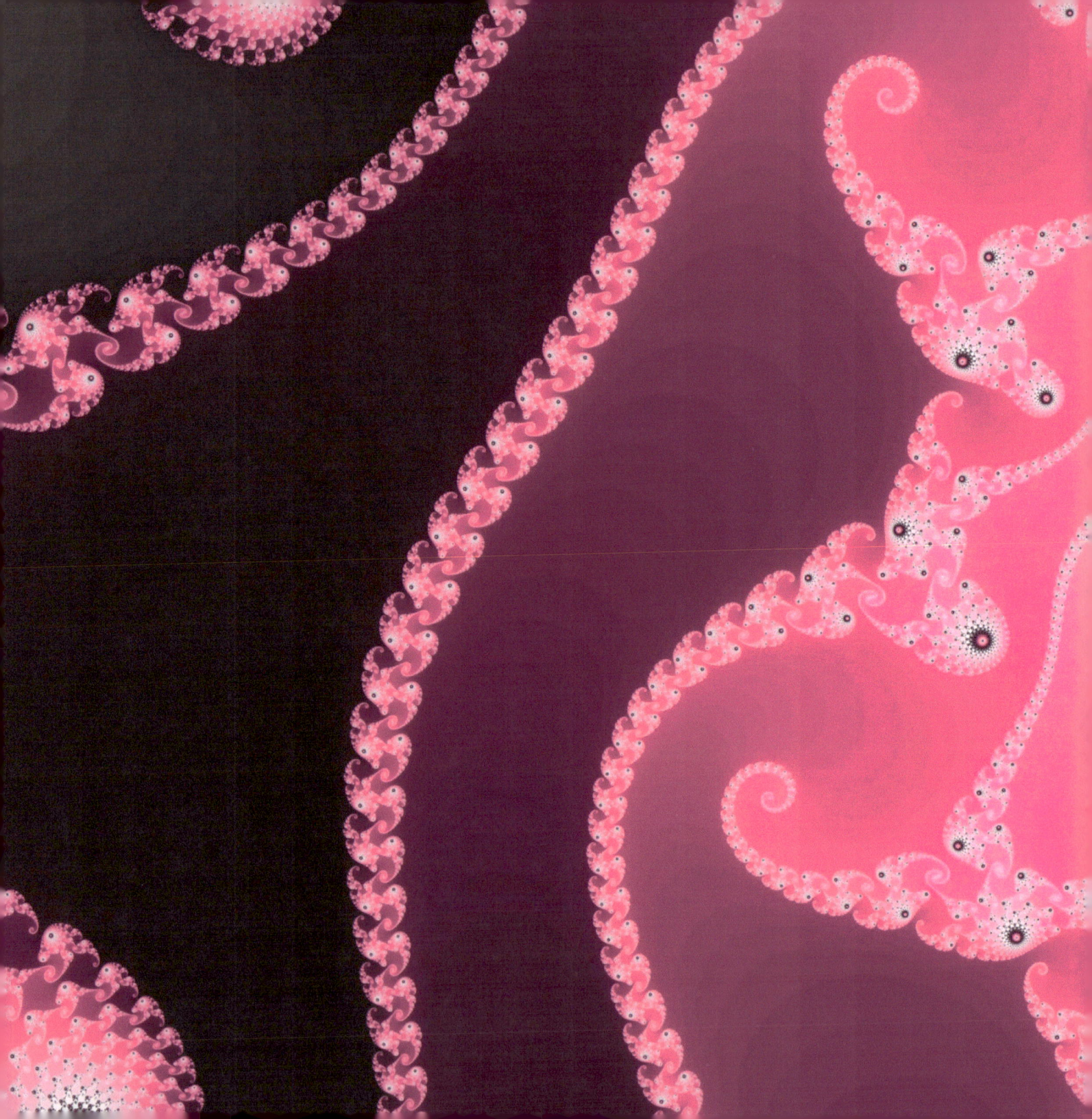

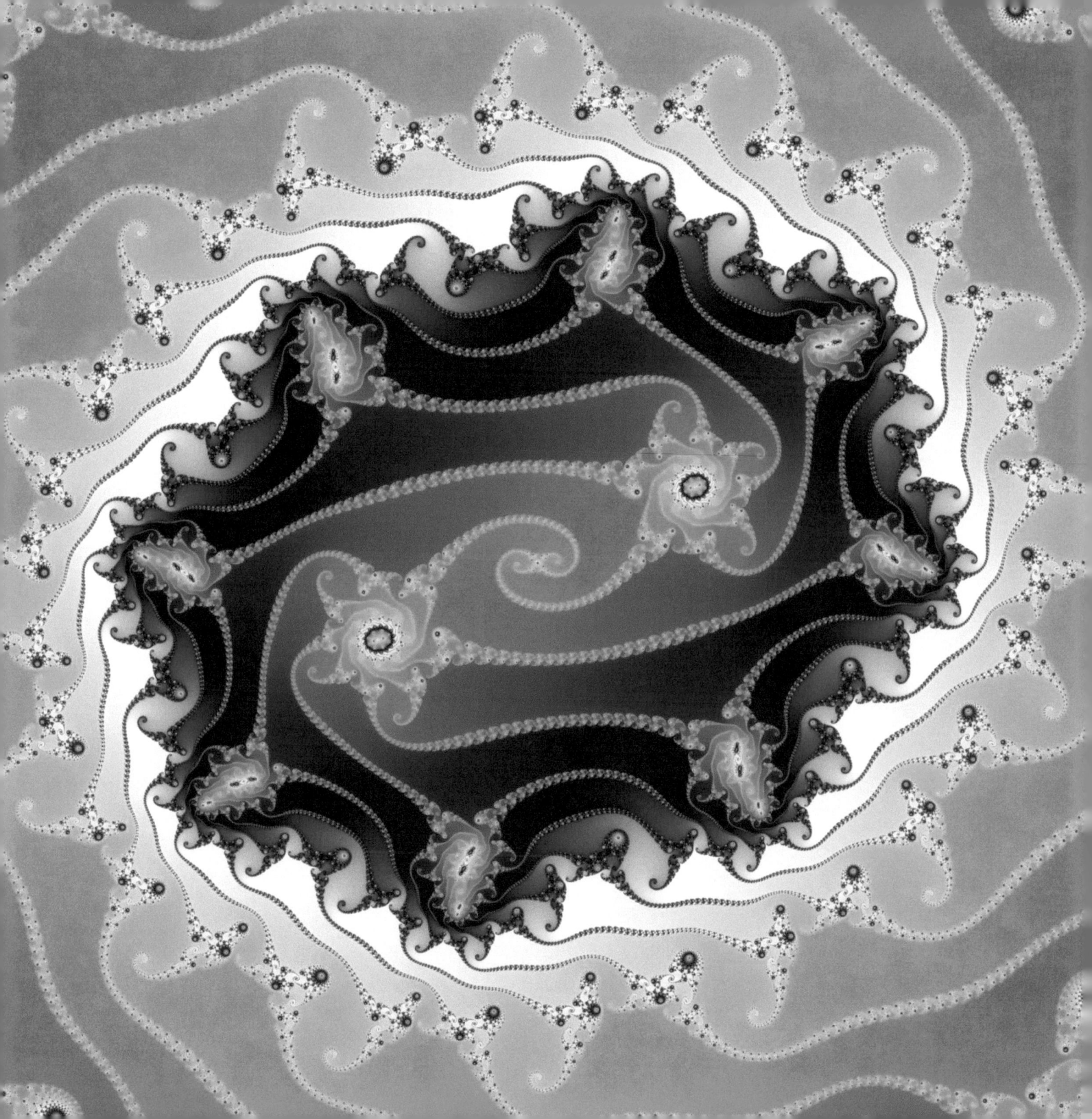

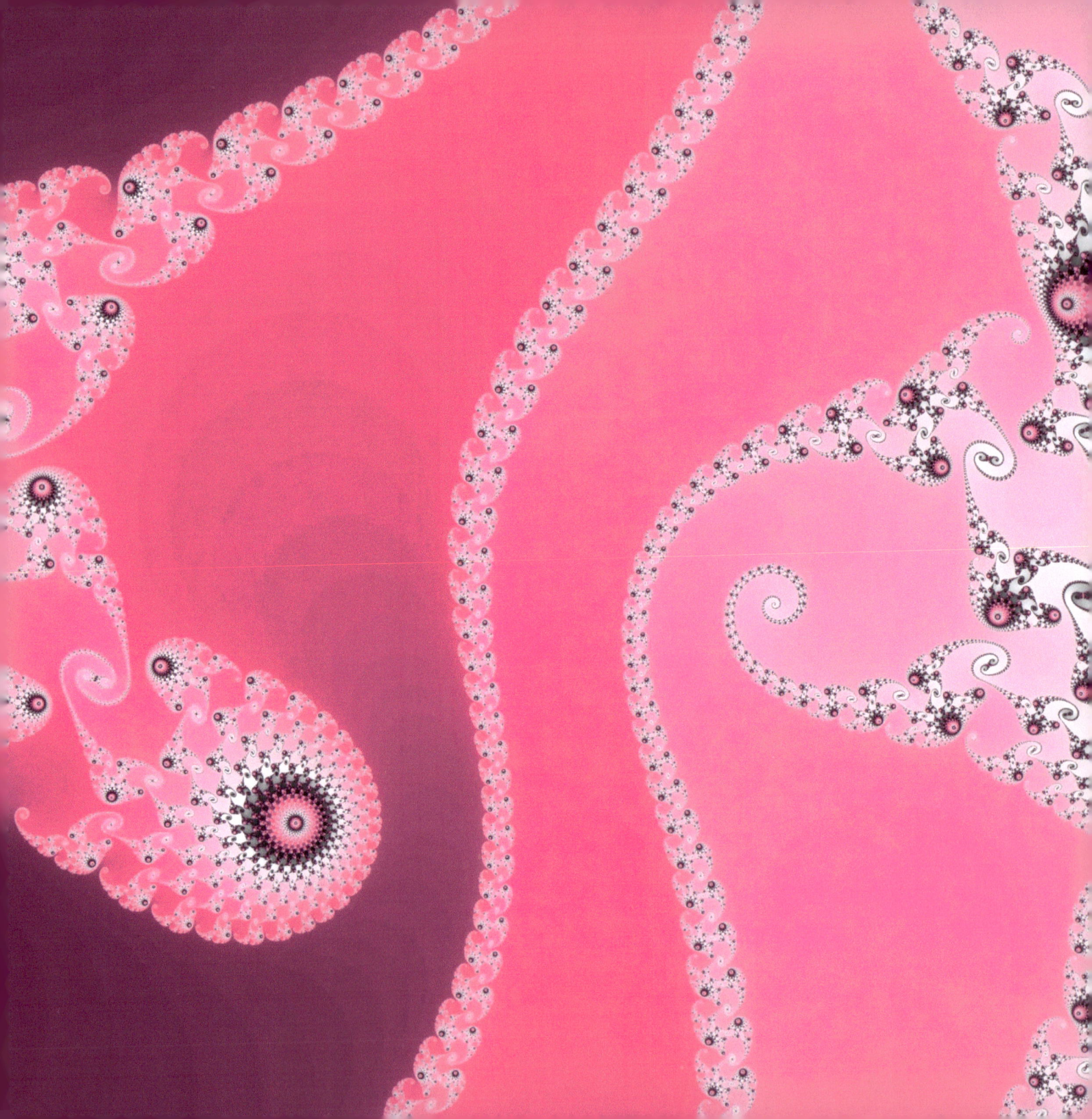

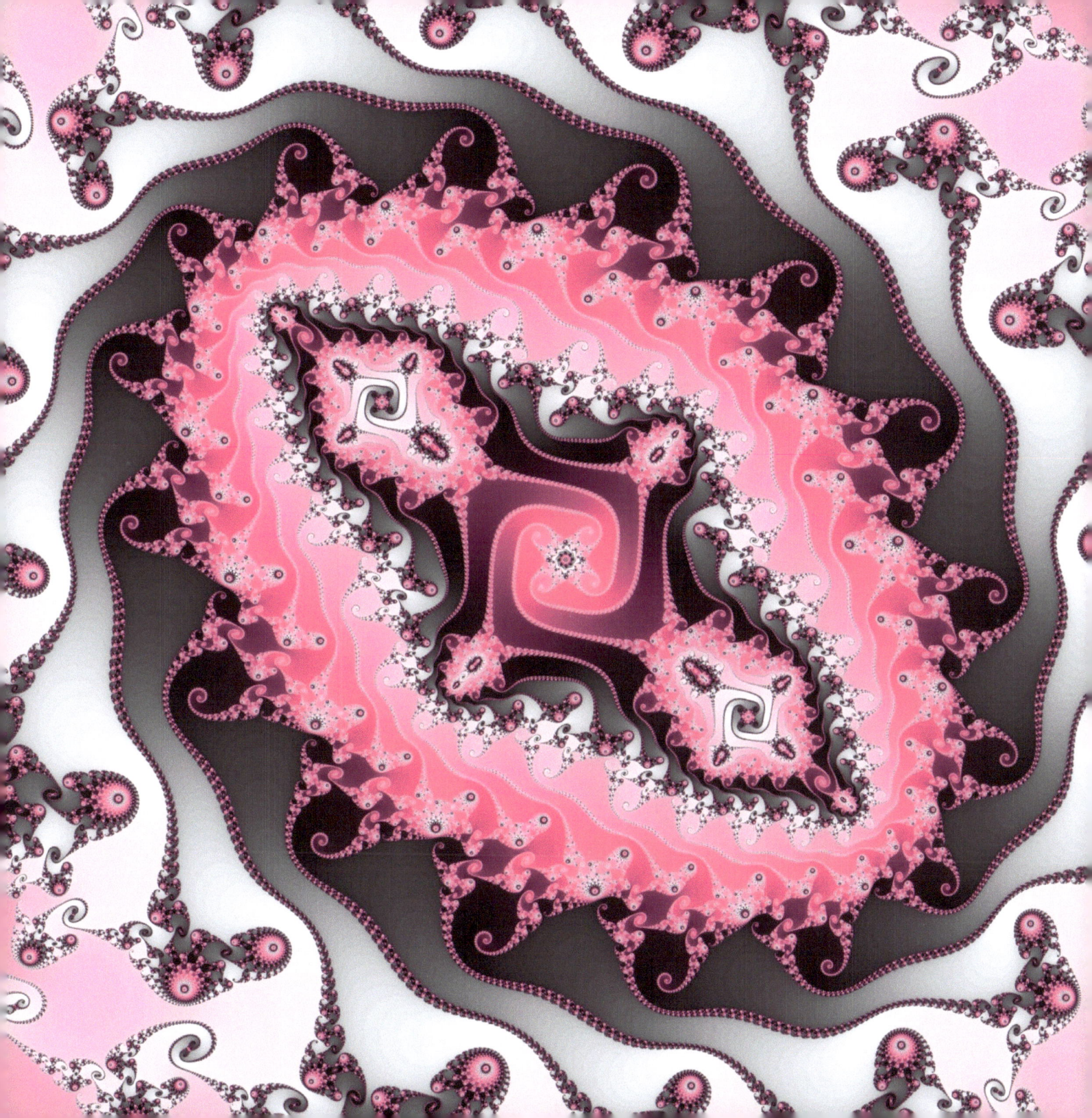

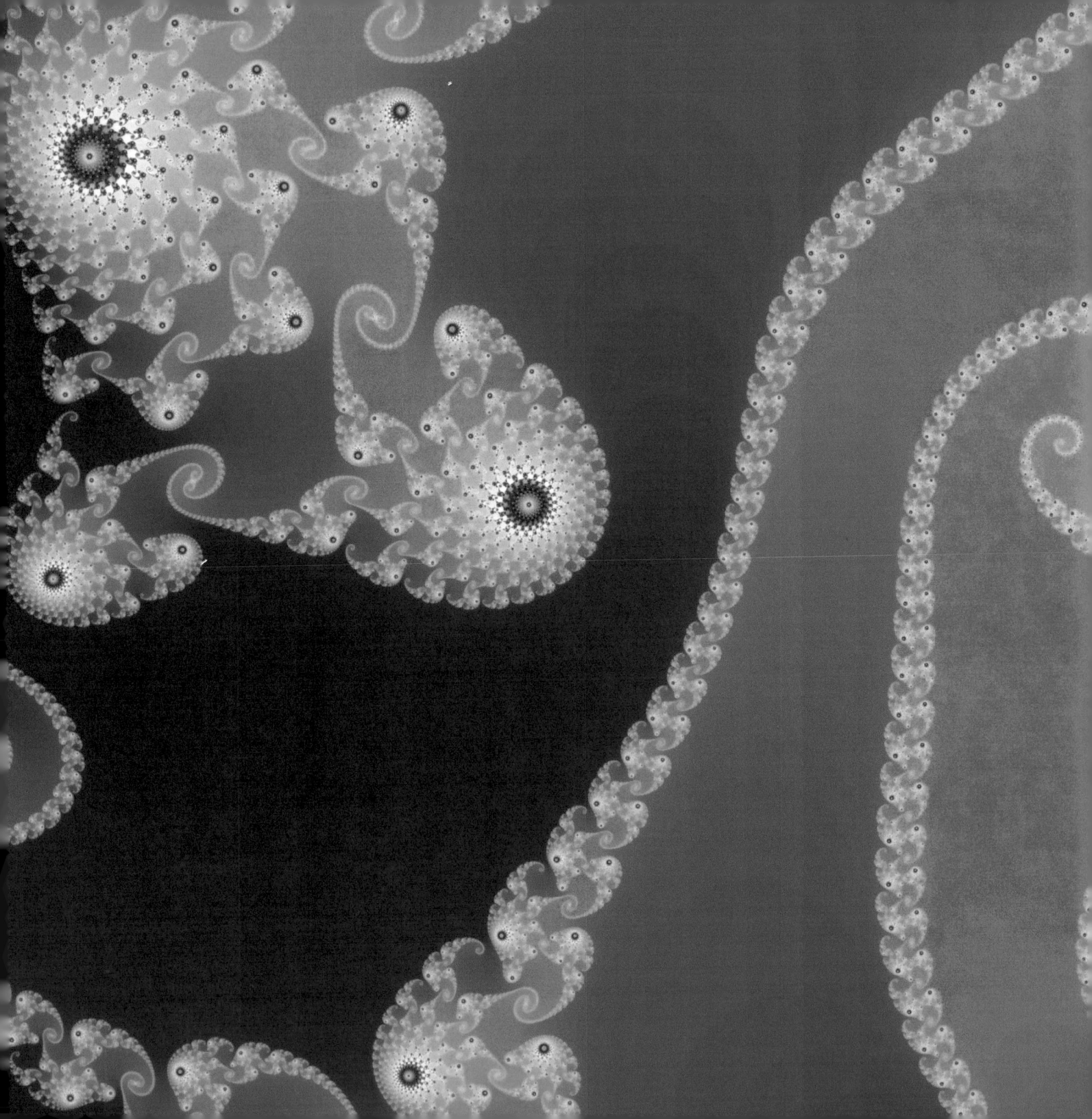

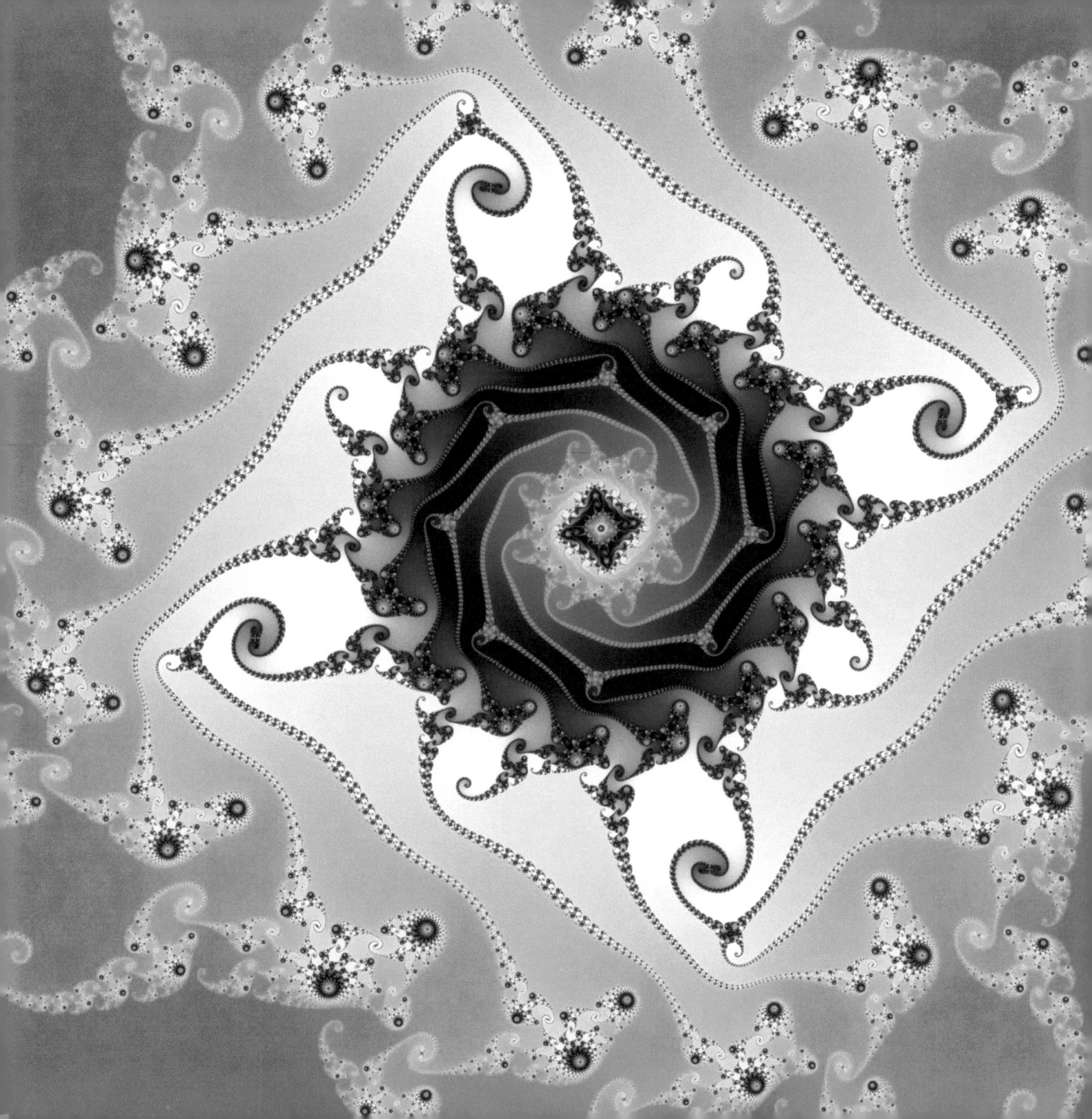

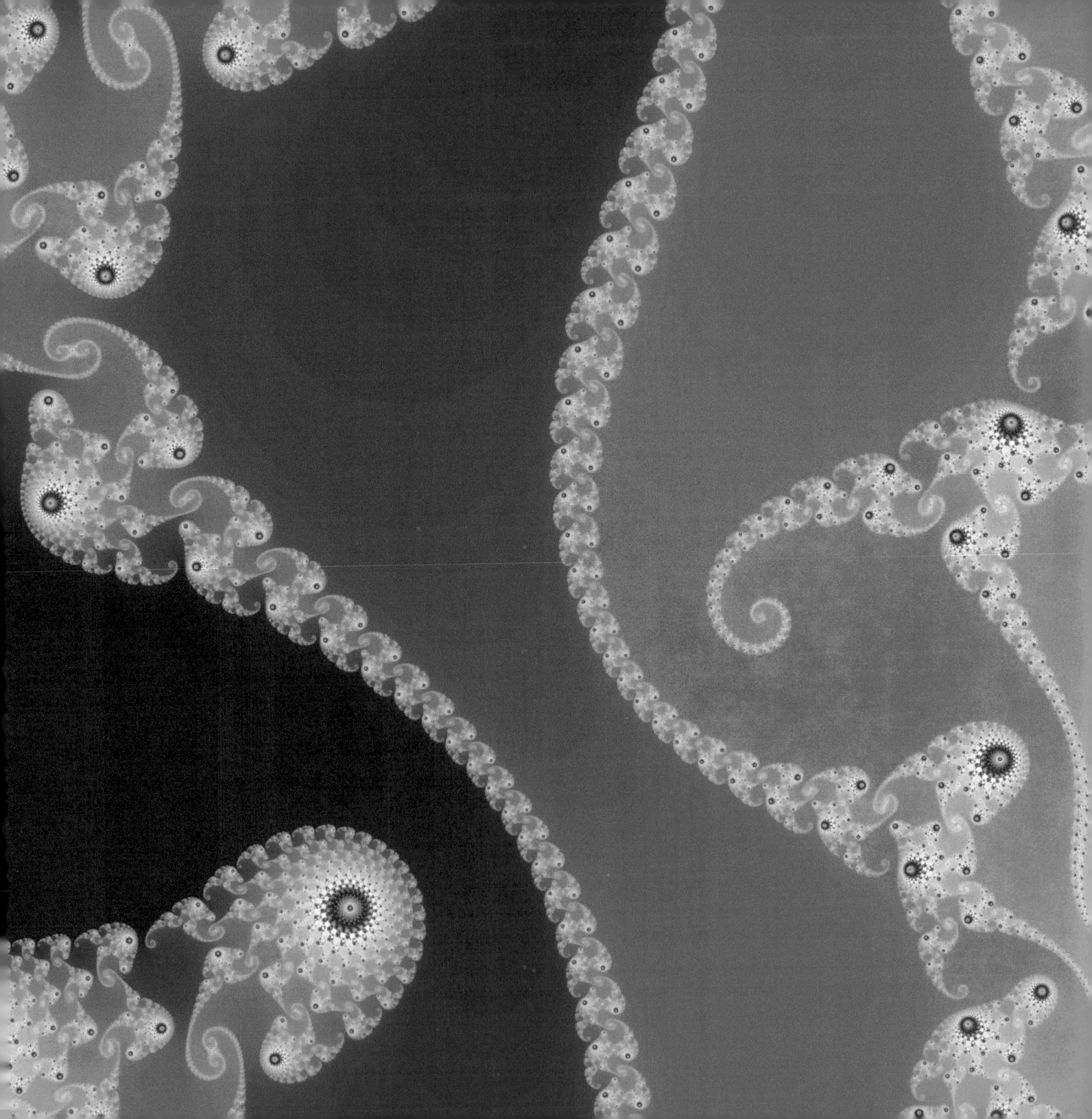

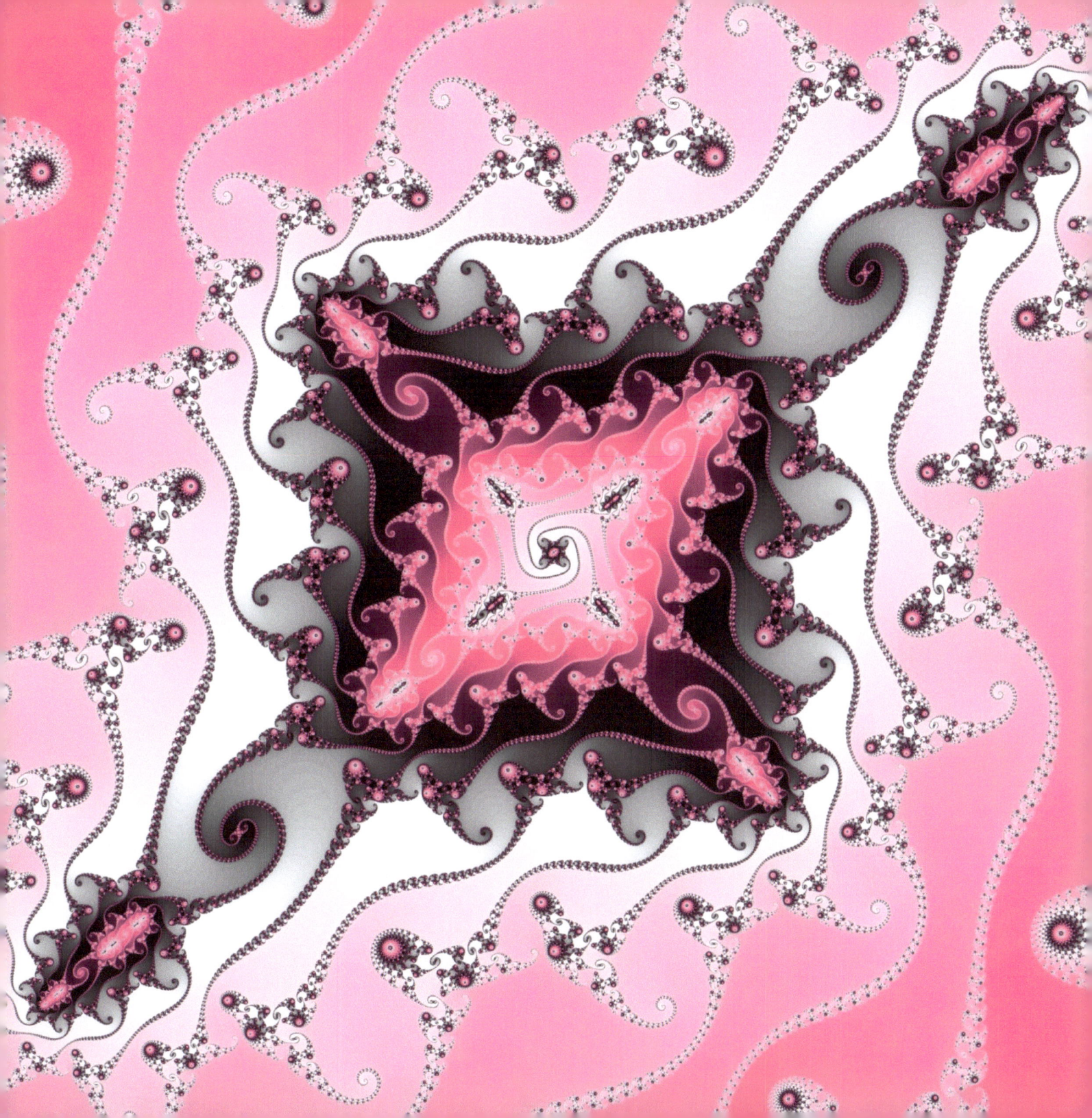

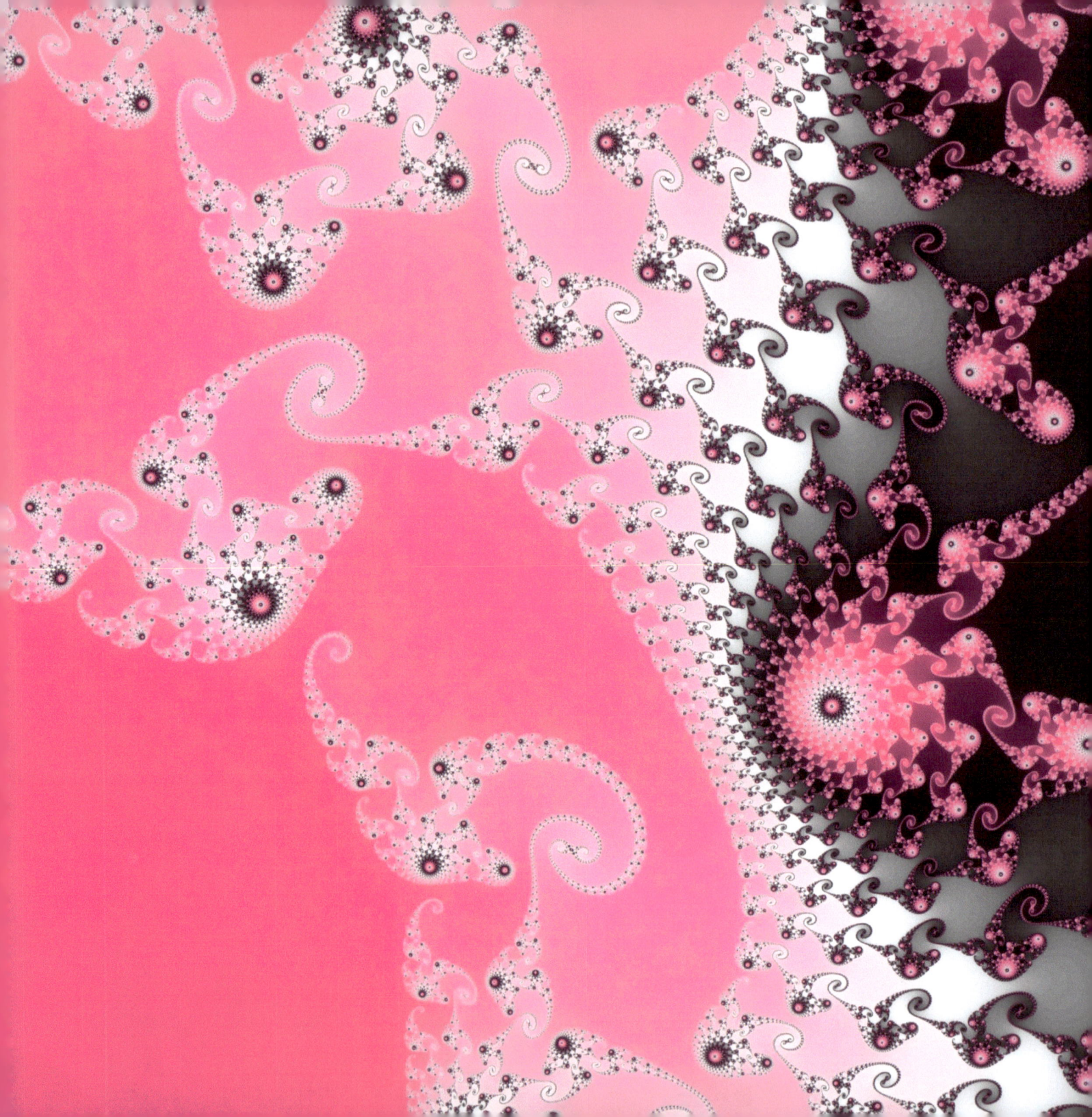

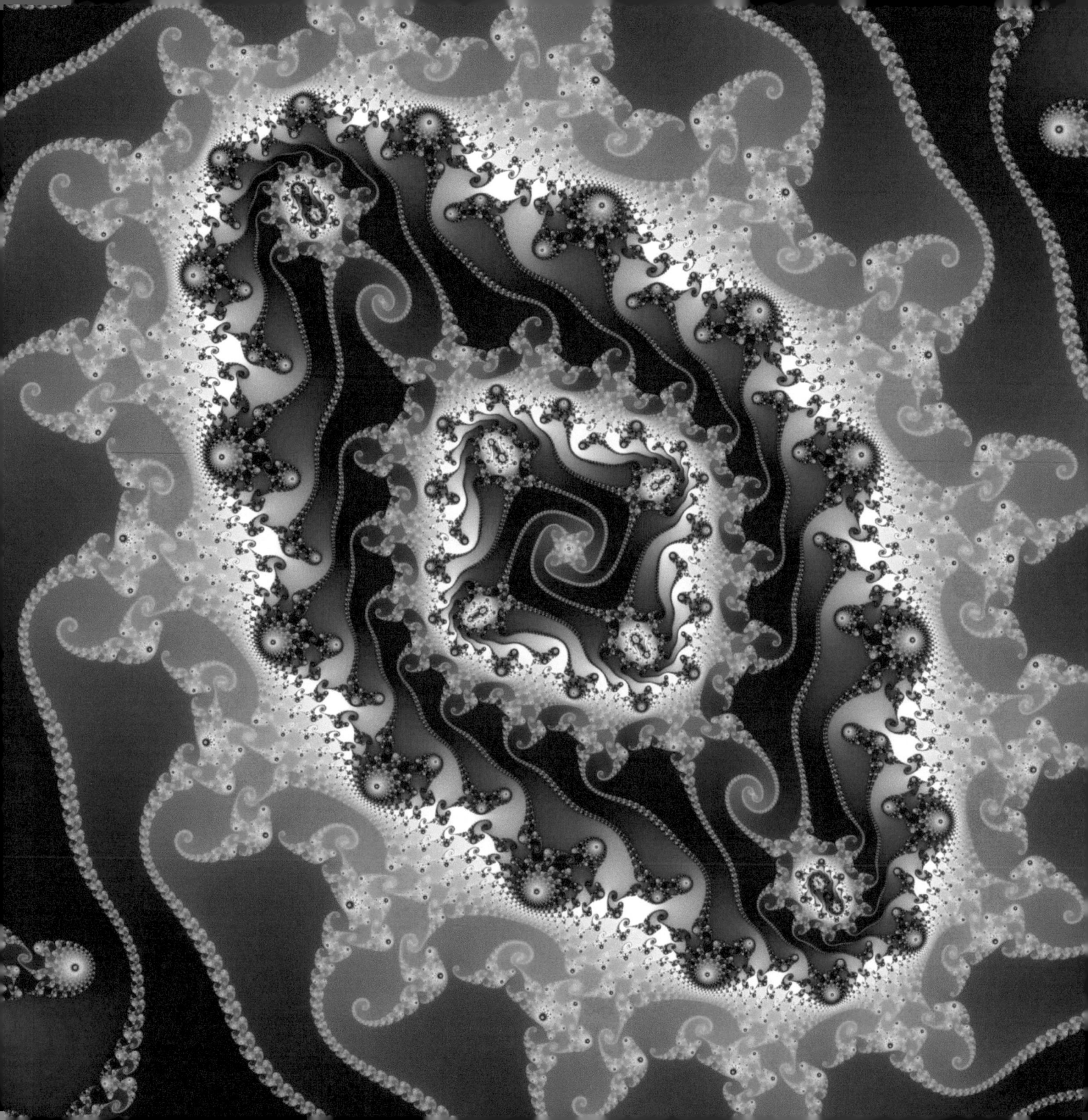

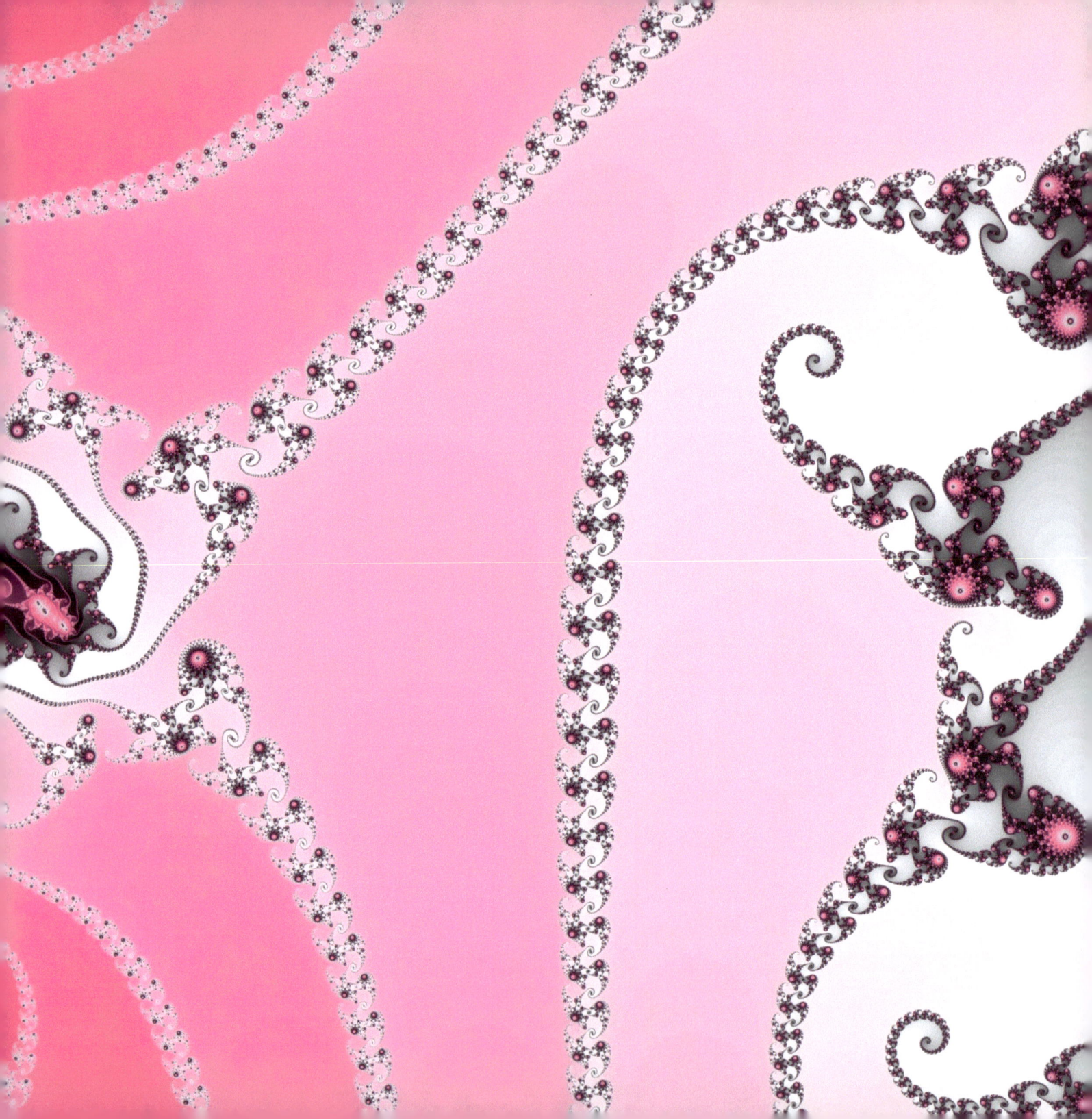

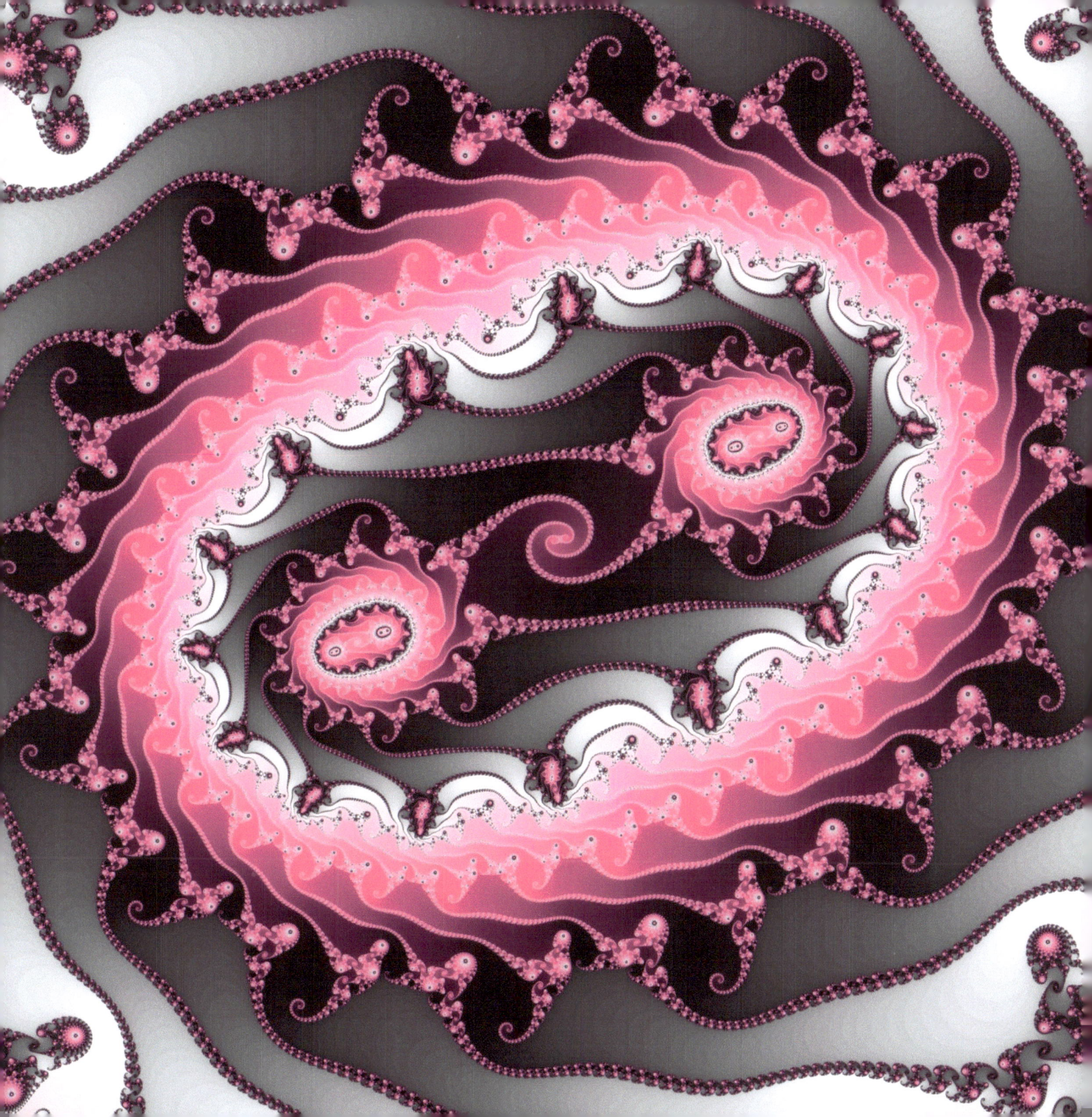

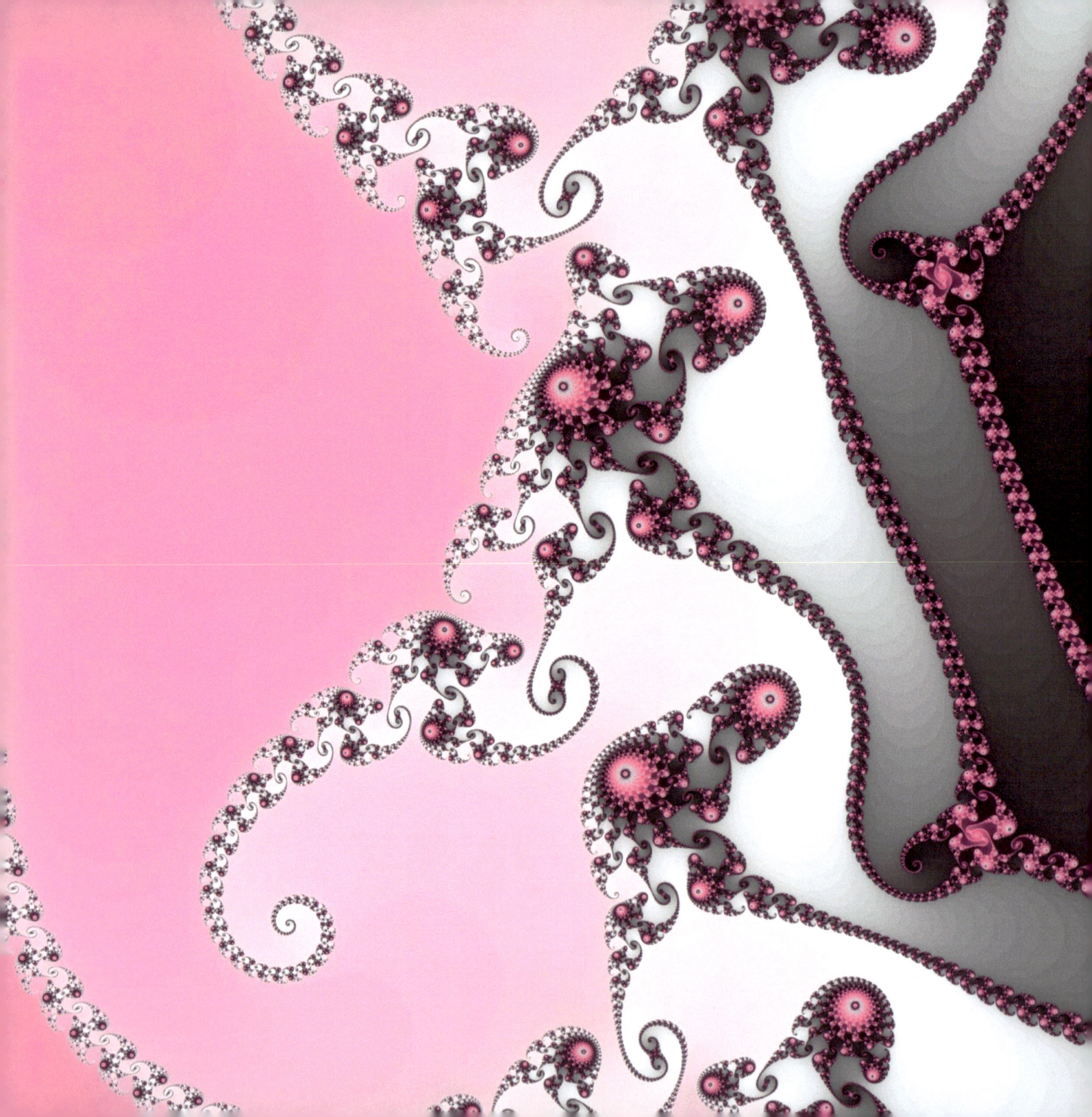

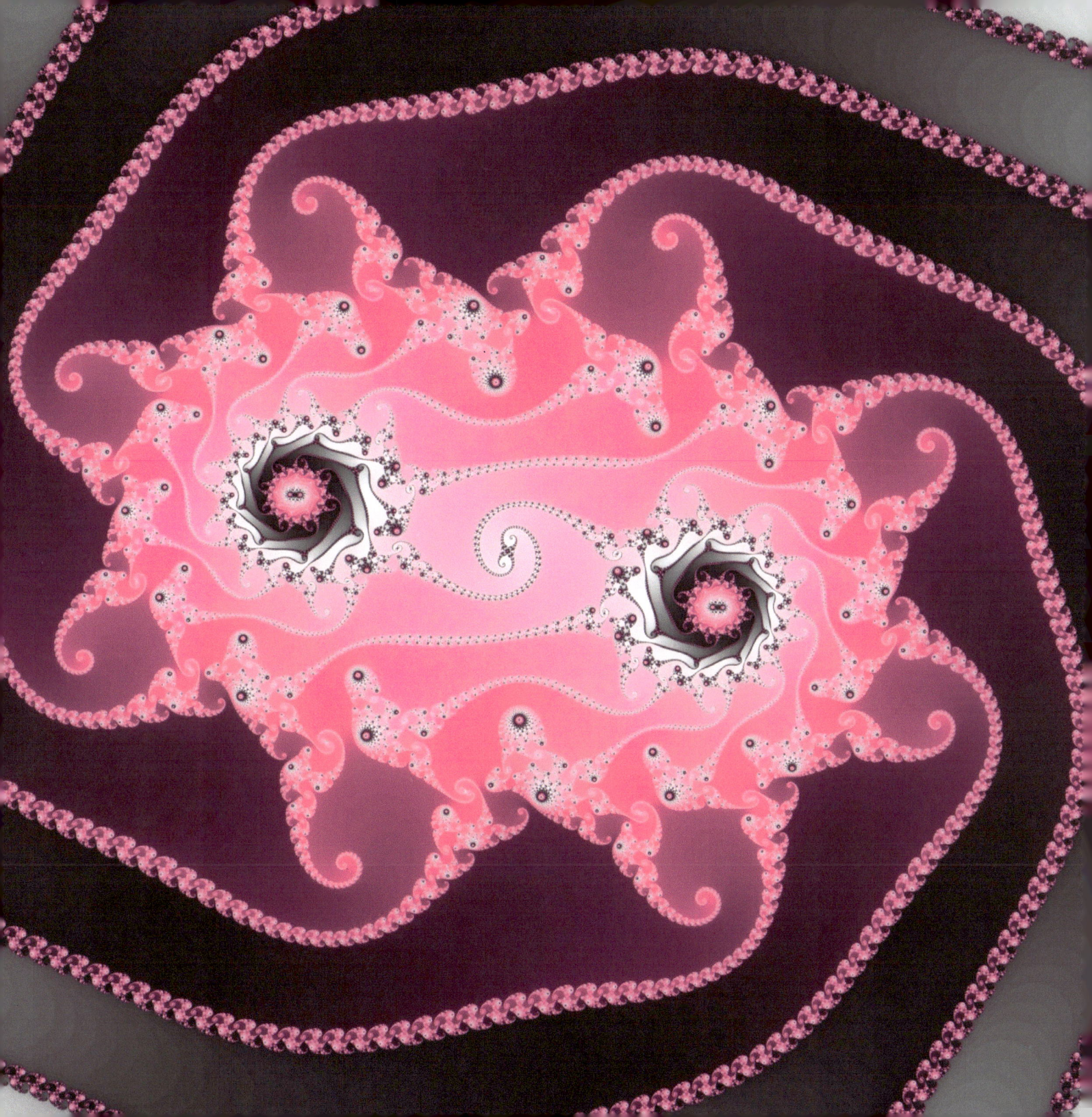

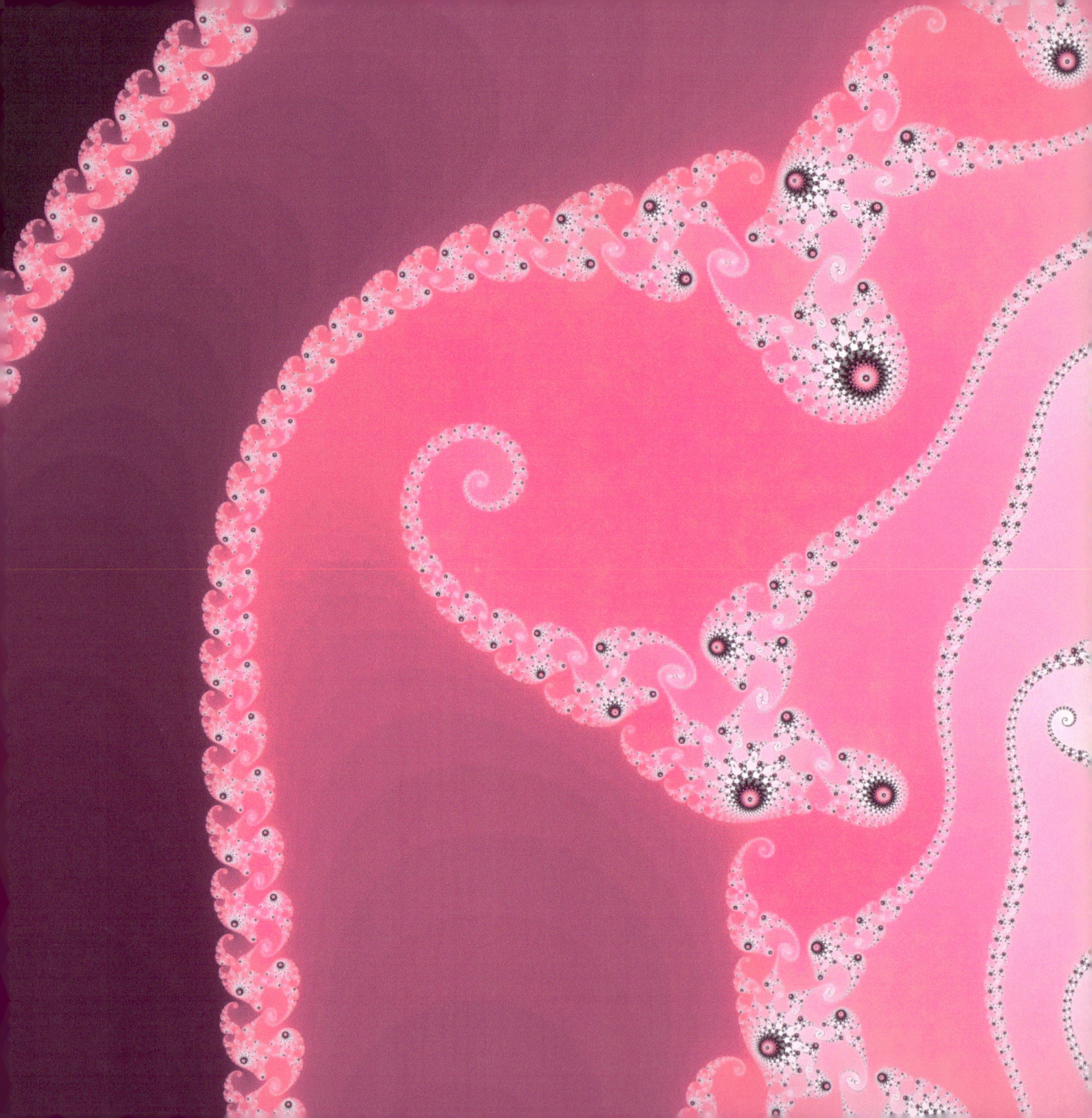

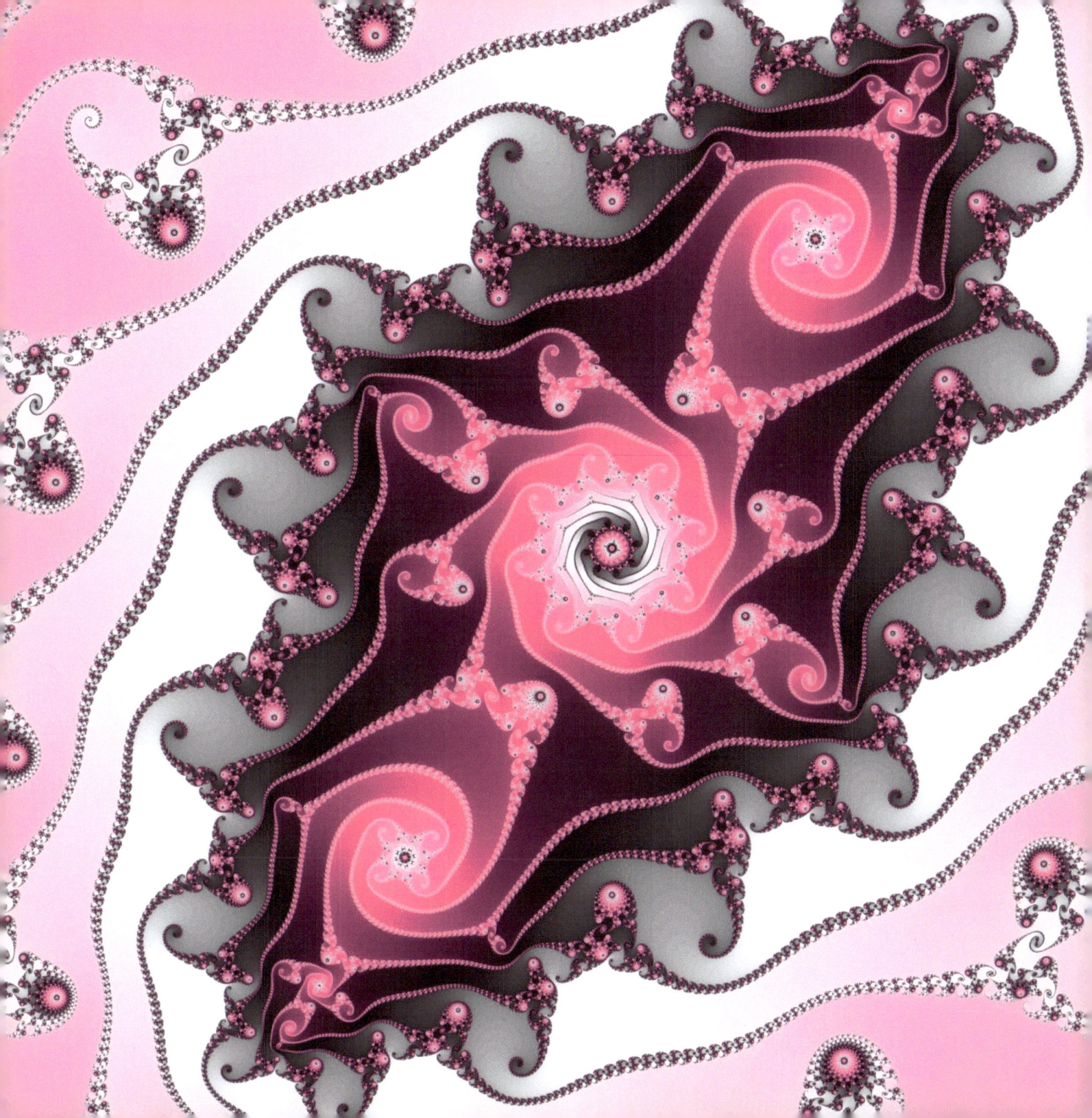

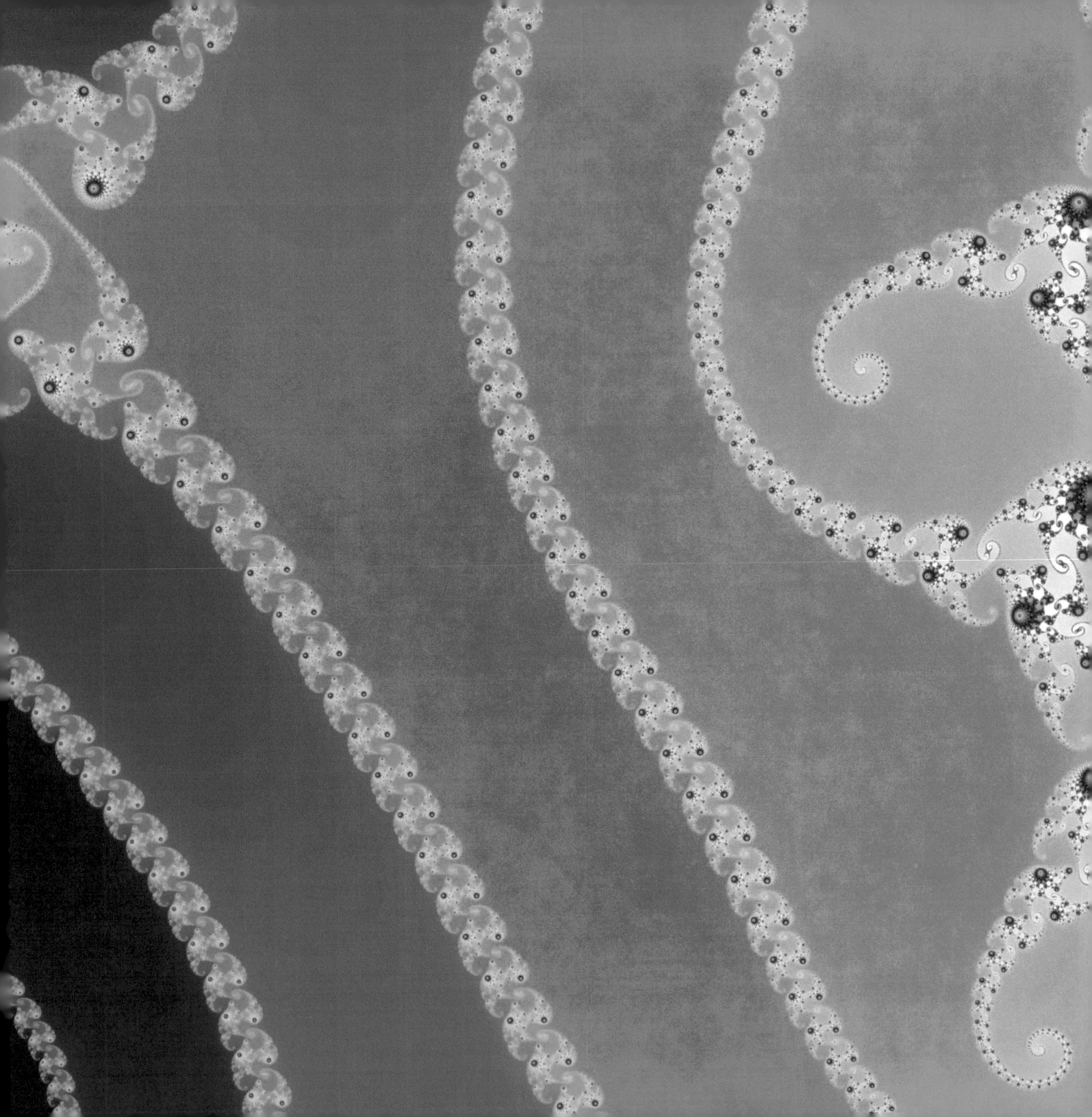

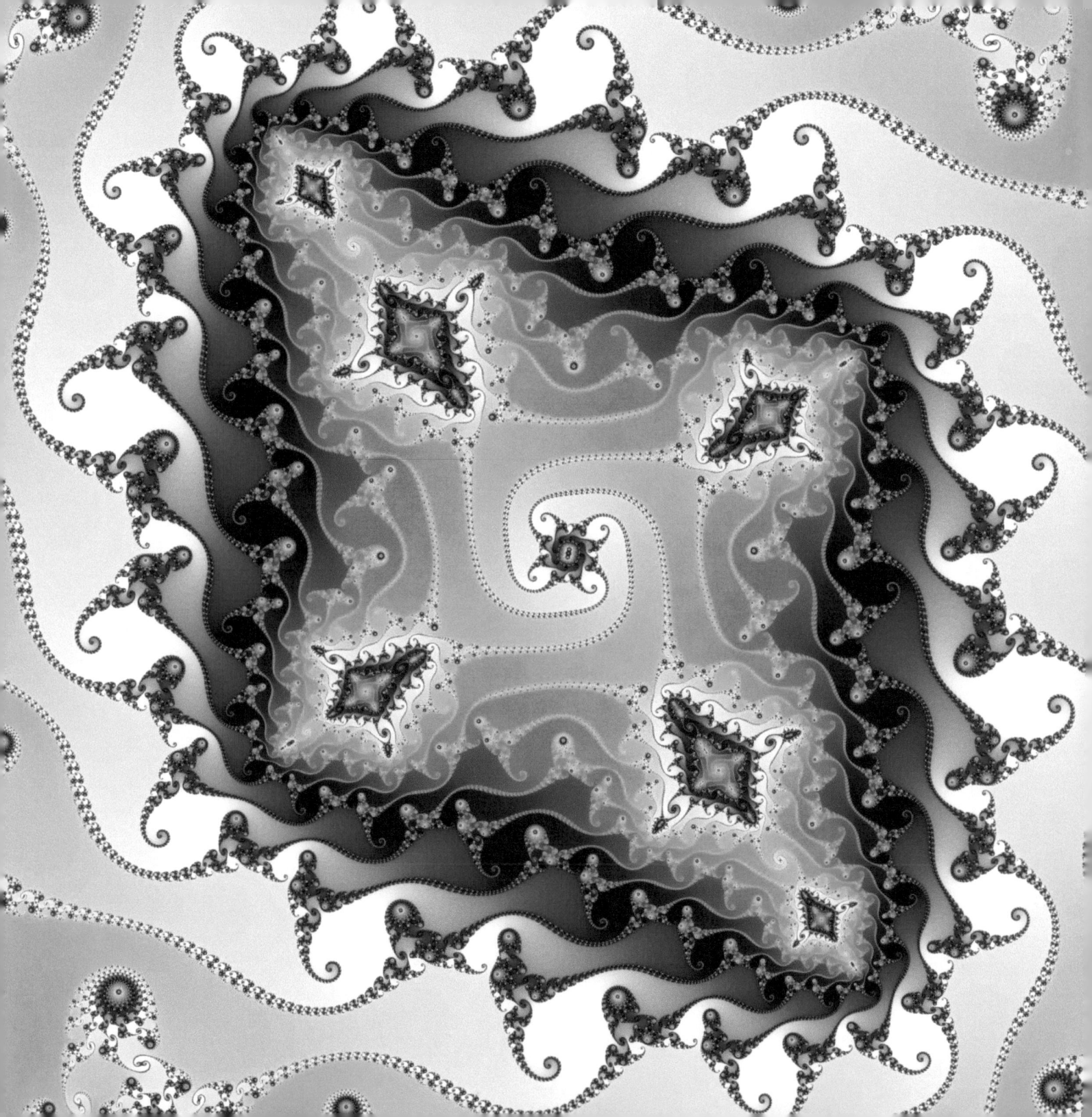

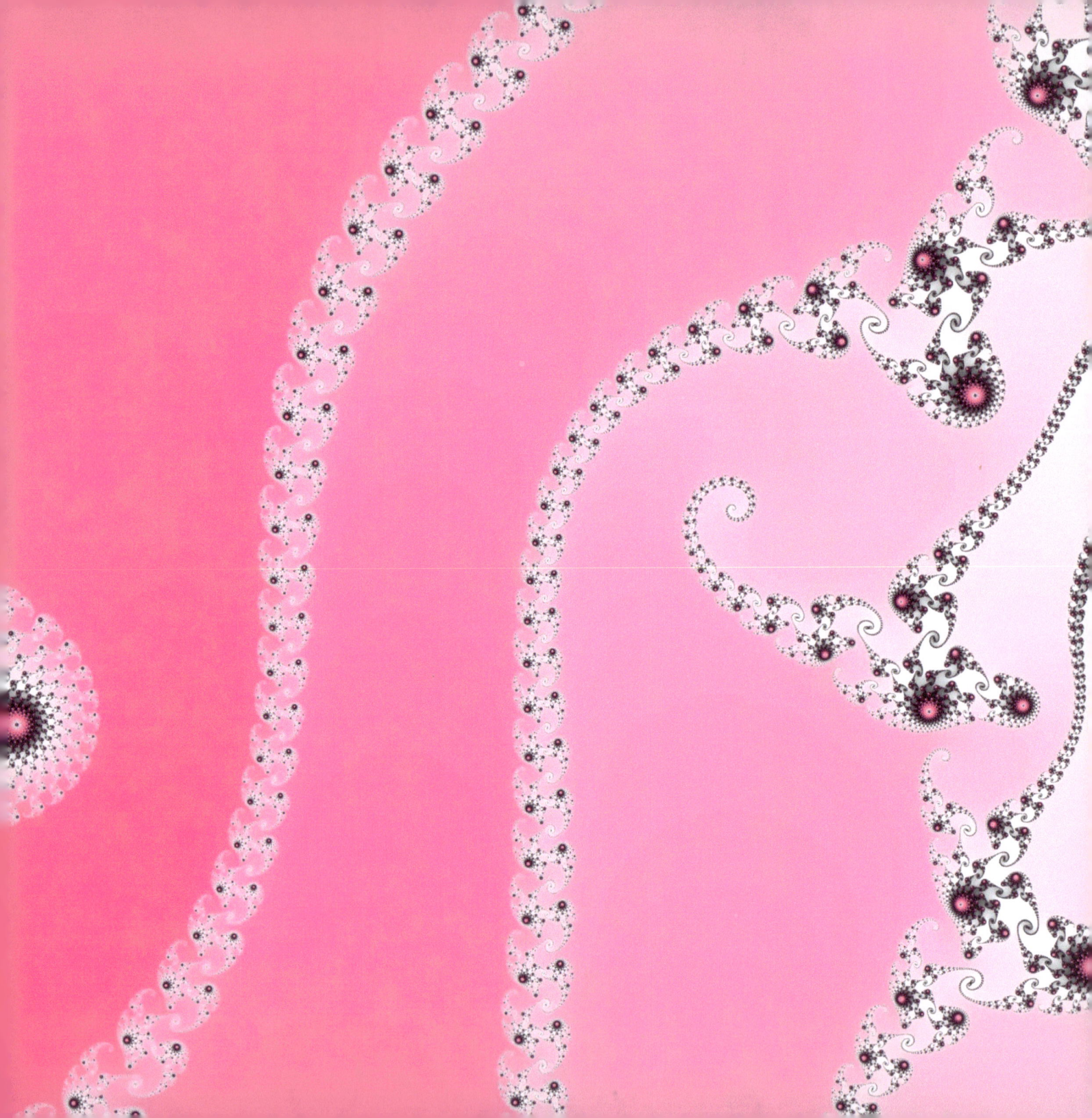

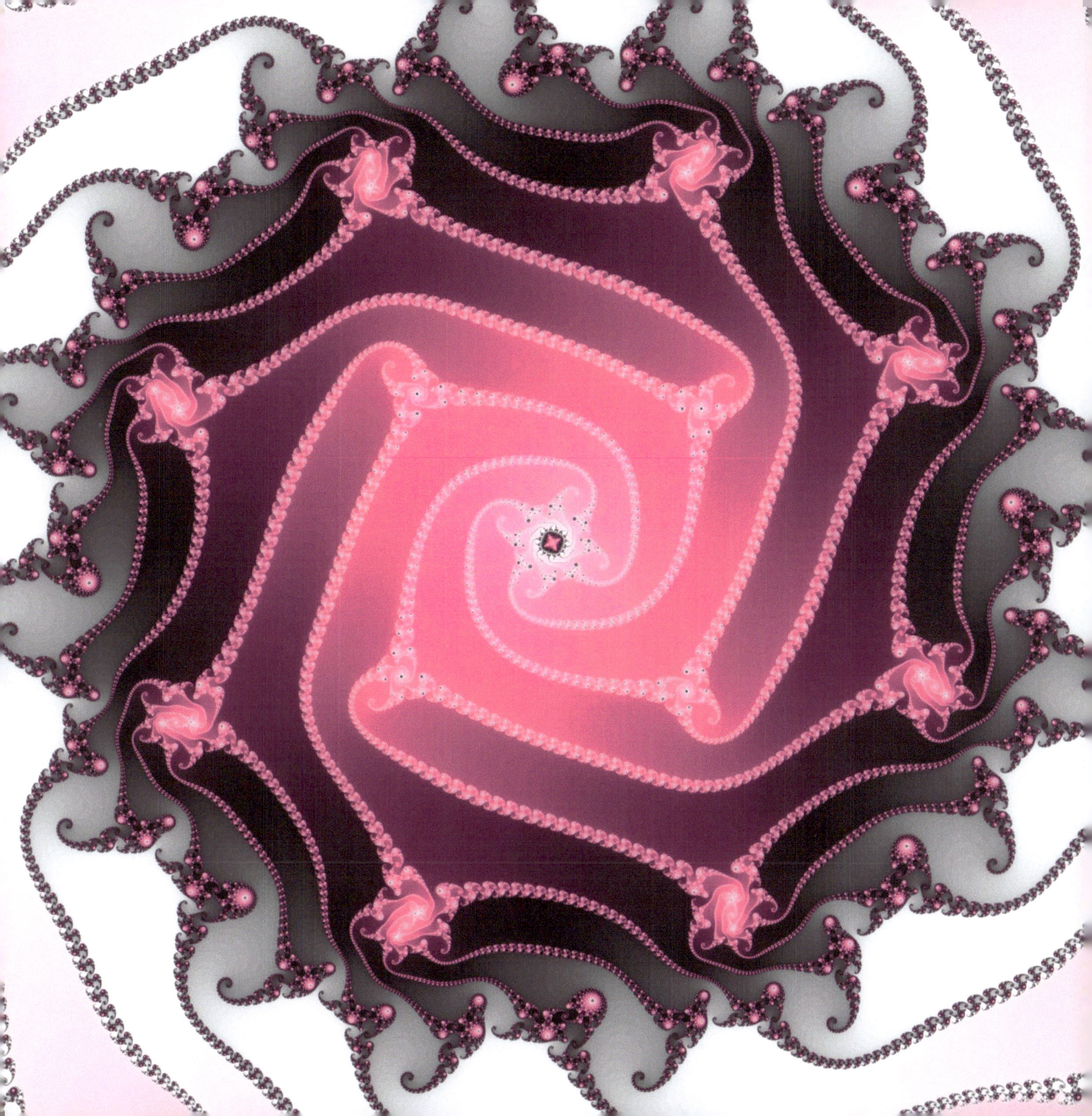

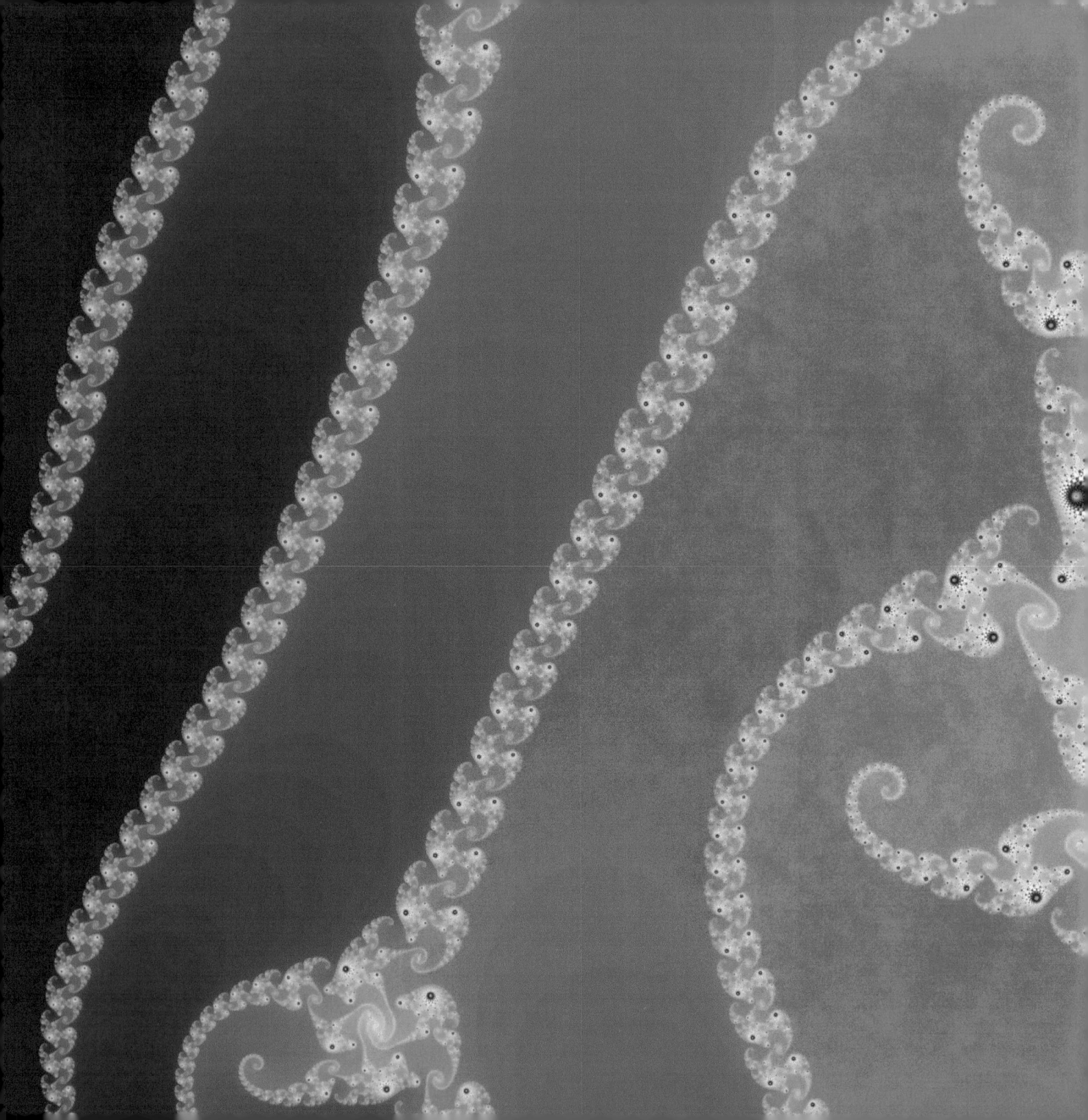

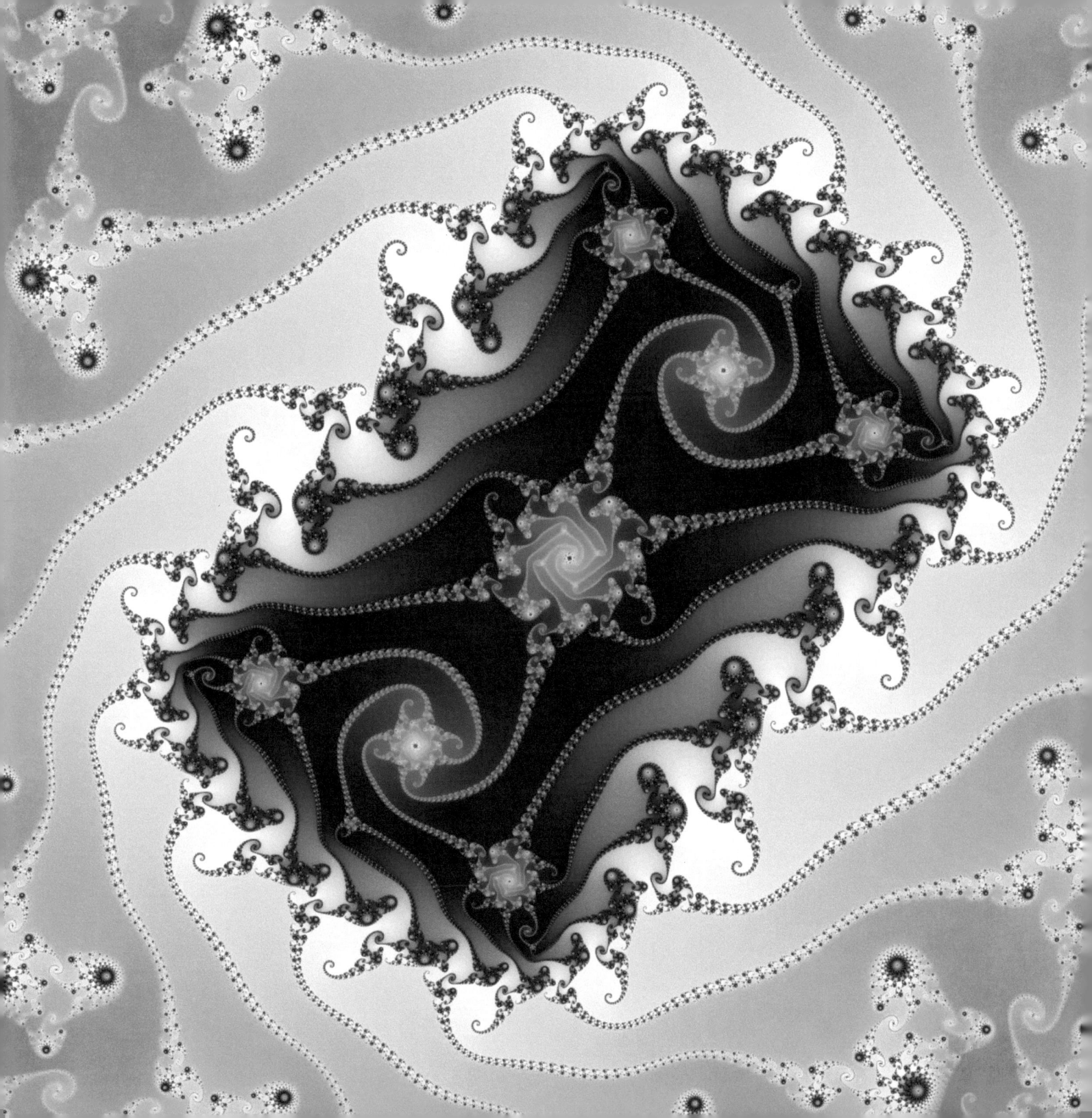

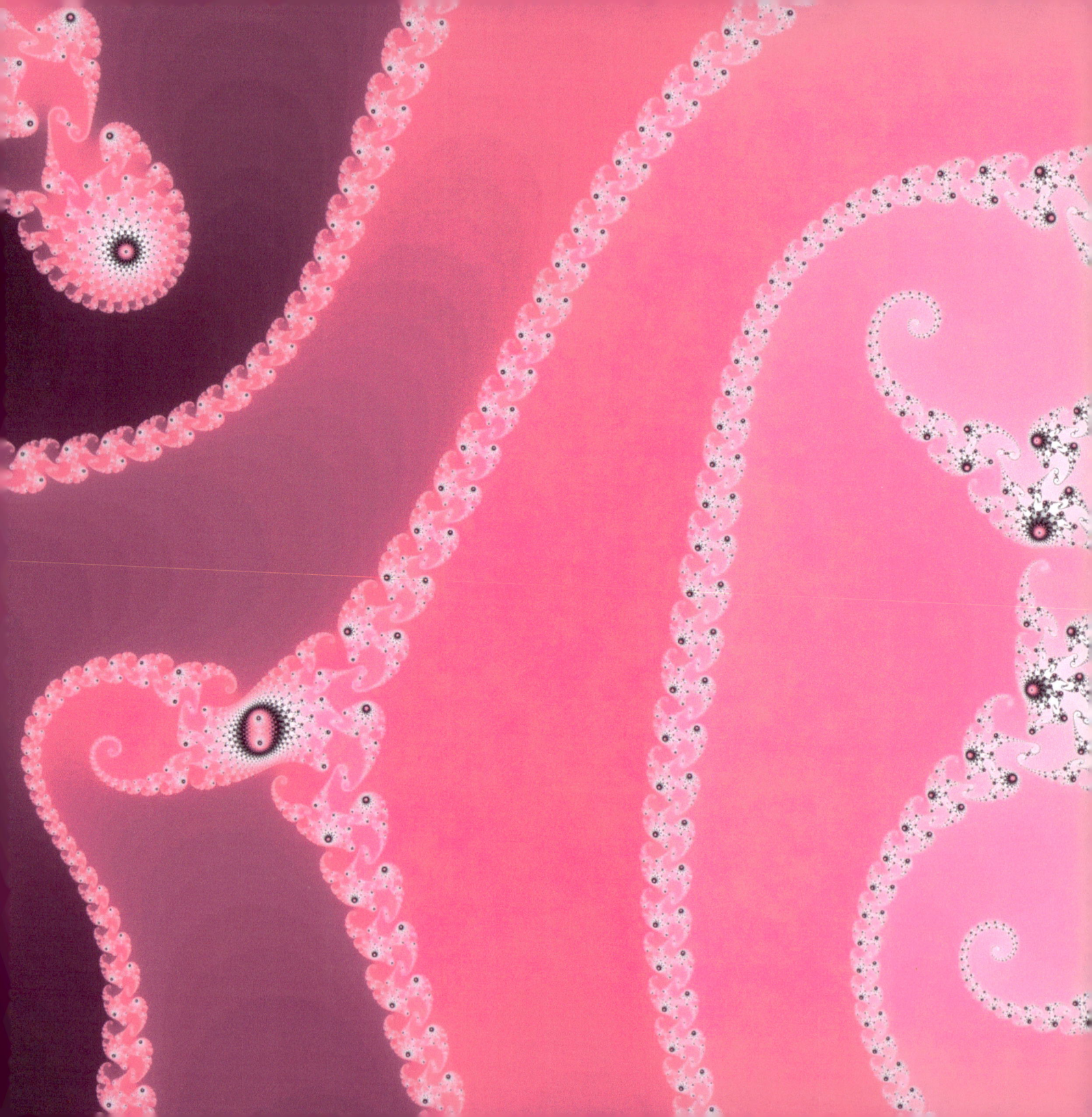

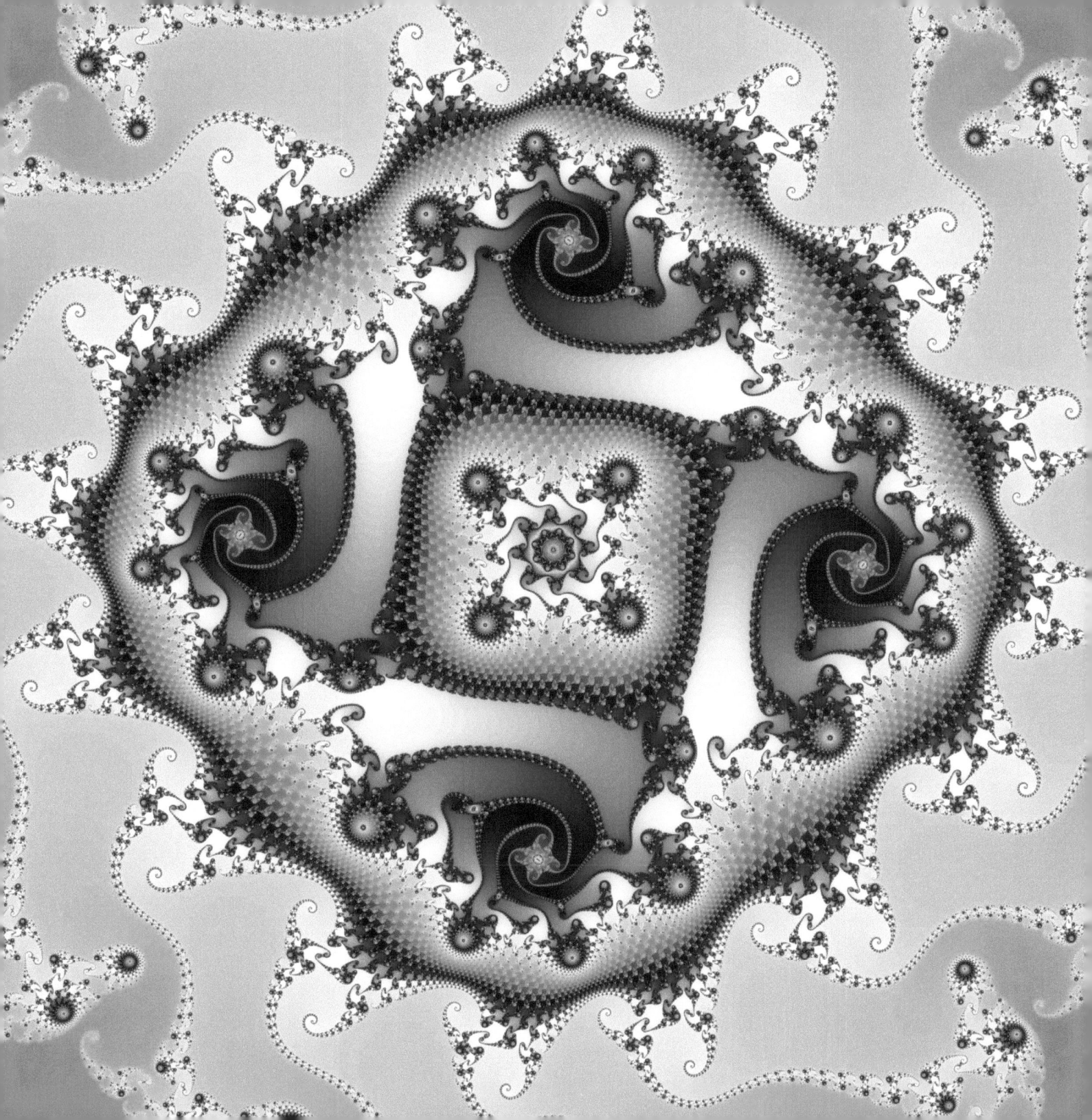

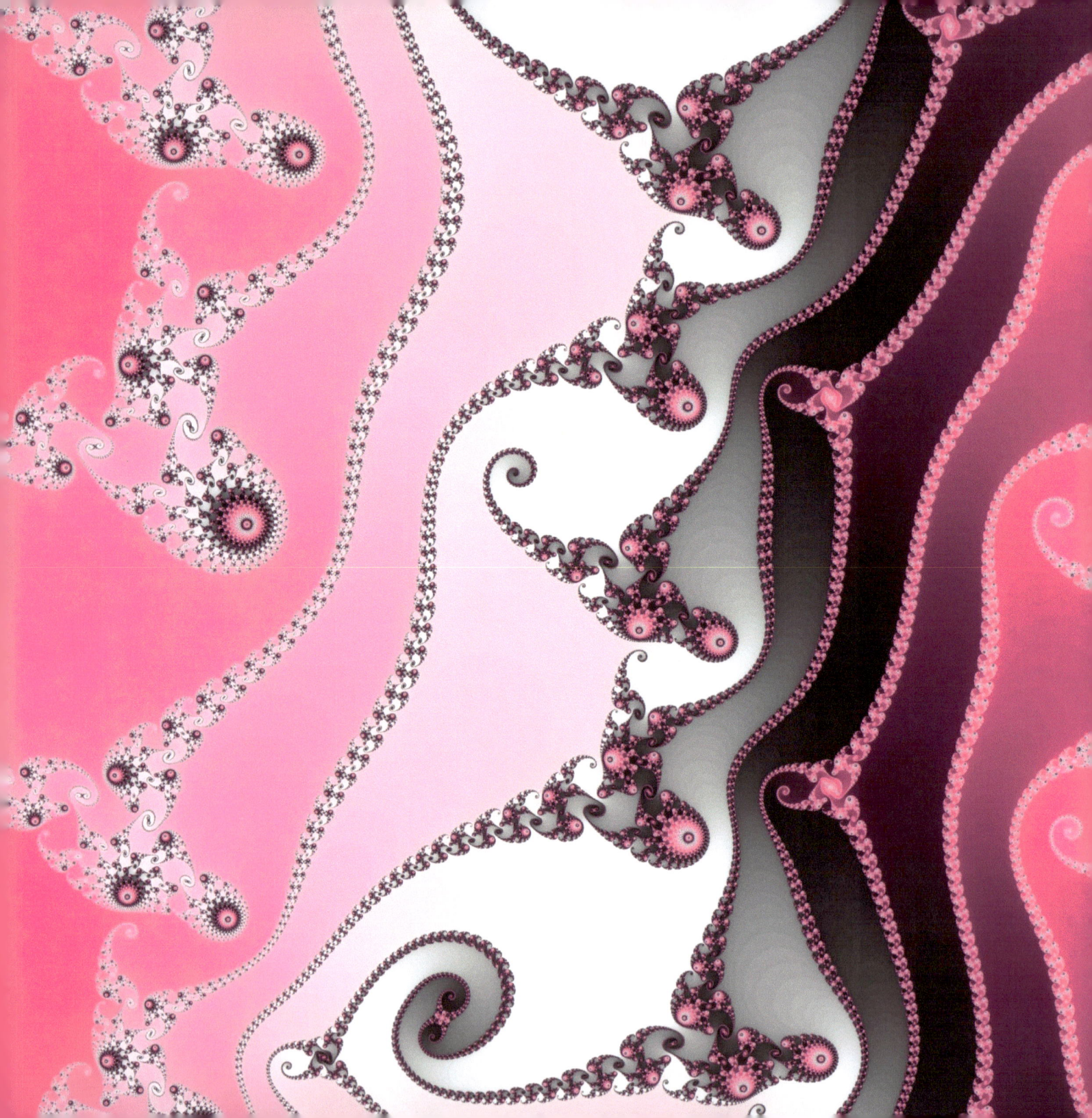

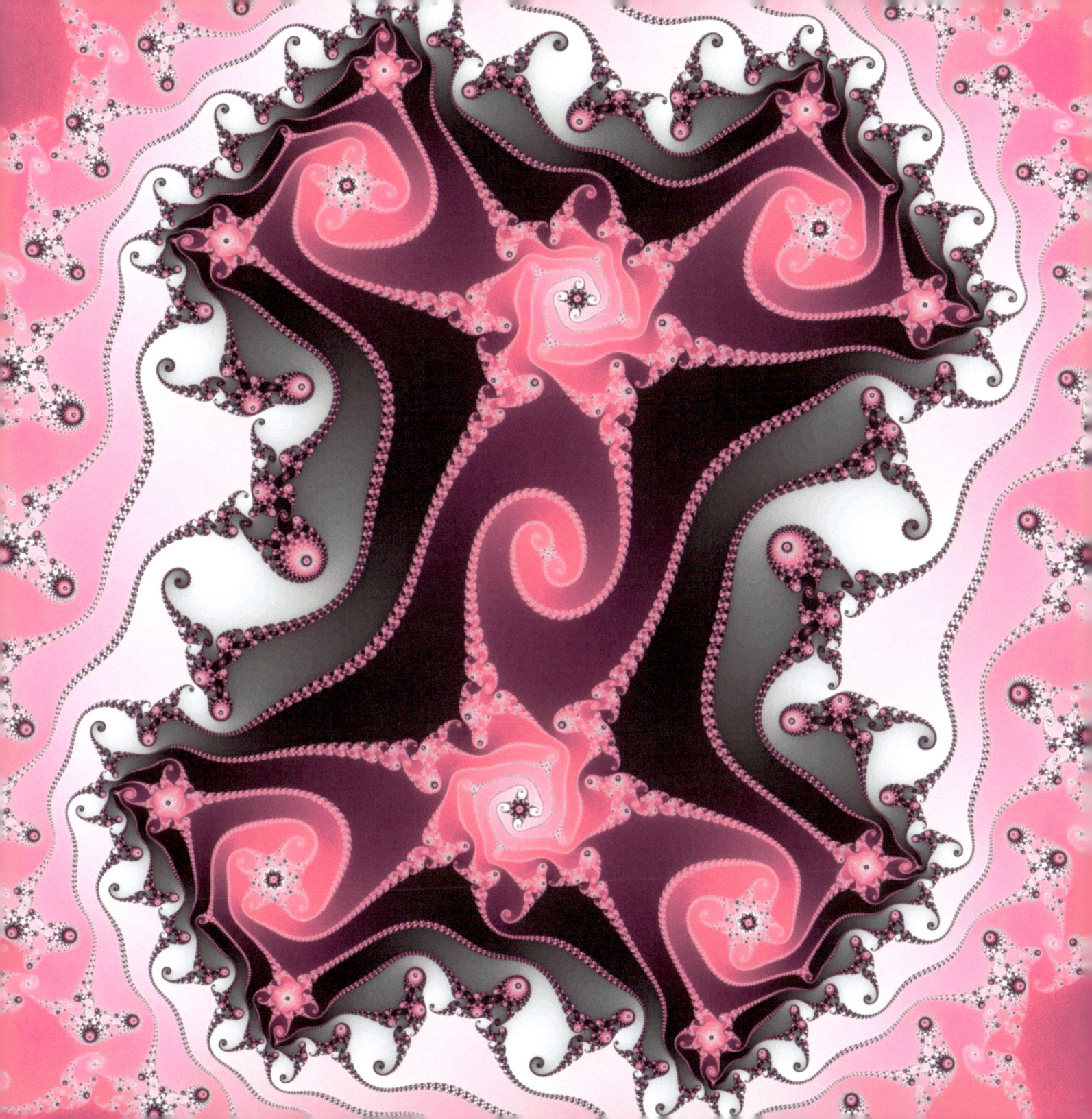

For more information visit

www.therapy4thought.com

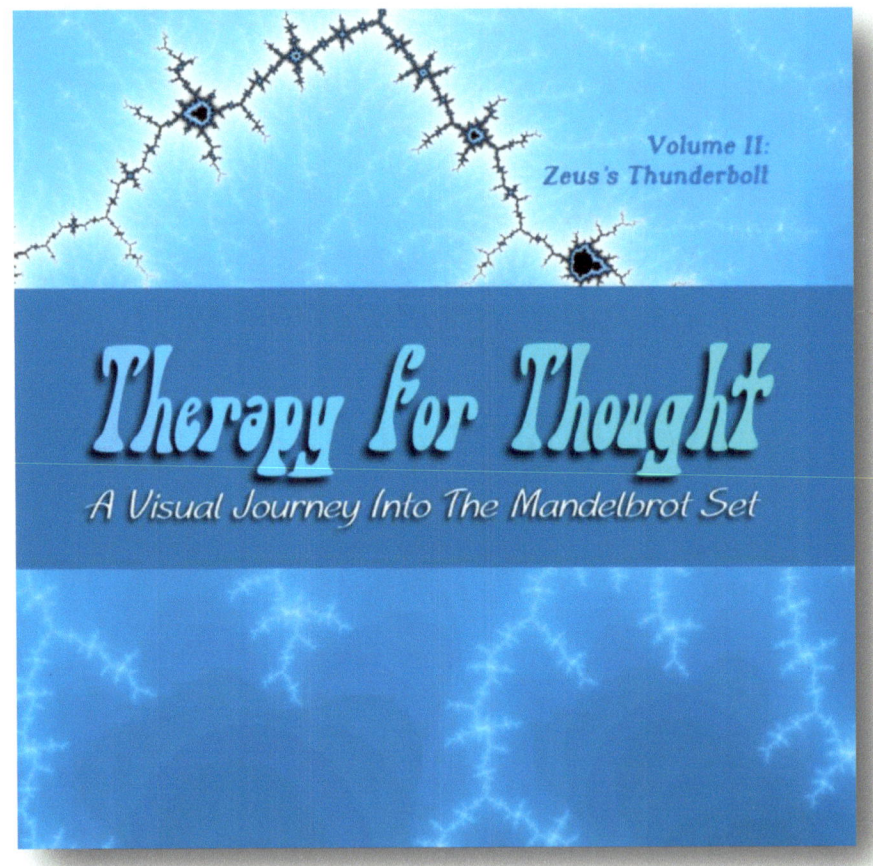

Volume II:
Zeus's Thunderbolt

Therapy for Thought

A Visual Journey Into The Mandelbrot Set

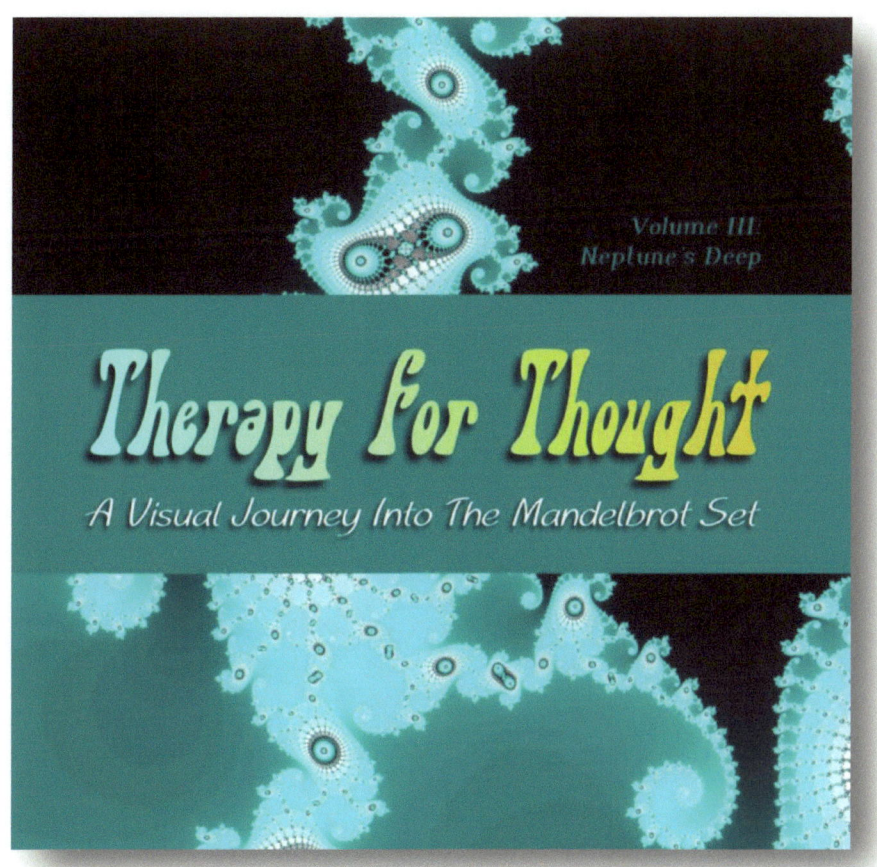

Volume III:
Neptune's Deep

Therapy for Thought

A Visual Journey Into The Mandelbrot Set

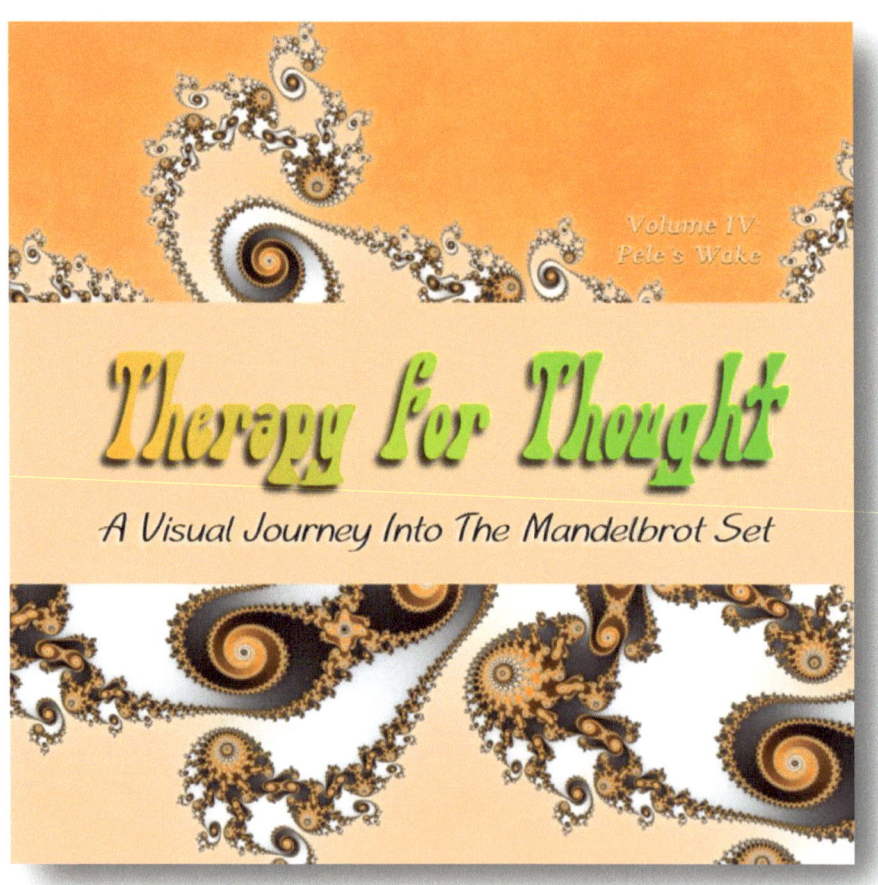

Volume IV:
Pele's Wake

Therapy For Thought

A Visual Journey Into The Mandelbrot Set

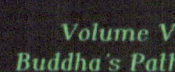

Volume V:
Buddha's Path

Therapy For Thought

A Visual Journey Into The Mandelbrot Set